# PRAISE FOR
# ANSWERING THE NEW ATHEISM

❦ ❧

"In a better world than ours there would have been no need for *Answering the New Atheism*. But under the circumstances, I'm grateful to Dr. Scott Hahn and Dr. Benjamin Wiker for their essential service in coolly, rationally taking apart Richard Dawkins' inflamed rhetoric and exposing the absurdities, and the dangers, at its heart. Their final chapter is a particularly chilling, important reminder of what Dawkins' secular faith would lead to if it were more widely embraced."

❦ David Klinghoffer ❧
Author of *Shattered Tablets: Why We Ignore the Ten Commandments at Our Peril* and
*Why the Jews Rejected Jesus: The Turning Point in Western History*

❦ ❧

"*Answering the New Atheism* is a superb exposé of Dawkins' *The God Delusion*. Systematically and lucidly, Scott Hahn and Benjamin Wiker dissect and dispose of the fundamental errors that riddle Dawkins' attempt to demonize the divine. Dawkins has declared a jihad against religion and his main weapons are diatribe and caricature. But the authors refuse to respond in kind and instead turn to reason, the one tool that Dawkins seems to disdain. As readable and humorous as it is rigorously reasoned, *Answering the New Atheism* is the best antidote in the marketplace for Dawkinitis."

❦ Roy Abraham Varghese ❧
Co-author with Antony Flew of *There Is a God: How the World's
Most Notorious Atheist Changed His Mind*, a book denounced by Dawkins.
Editor of *Cosmos, Bios, Theos*, a work with 24 Nobel Prize winners
that was described by *Time Magazine* as "the year's most intriguing book on God."

❦

D0047249

i

~: :~

"Scott Hahn and Benjamin Wiker patiently, thoroughly pick apart the reasoning of Richard Dawkins until very little is left standing. I highly recommend *Answering the New Atheism* to anyone who wants to watch scientific atheist bullies get their comeuppance."

~: Michael J. Behe :~
Lehigh University, Author of *The Edge of Evolution*

~: :~

"When two Catholic intellectual heavyweights collaborate on a project, expectations are high. Scott Hahn and Benjamin Wiker, scholars and best-selling authors, do not disappoint us in *Answering the New Atheism*. As co-authors they have produced a gem—a book that provides a clear response to the atheistic secularism of Richard Dawkins. In a logical, measured, and accessible manner they provide the reader with what is needed 'to give an answer to everyone who asks you to give the reason for the hope that you have . . . [doing so] with gentleness and respect' (1 Pet. 3:15–16)."

~: Regis J. Flaherty :~
Author of *Last Things First*

~: :~

# ANSWERING THE NEW ATHEISM

## DISMANTLING DAWKINS' CASE AGAINST GOD

~: :~

BY

SCOTT HAHN AND BENJAMIN WIKER

EMMAUS
ROAD
PUBLISHING

Emmaus Road Publishing
827 North Fourth Street
Steubenville, Ohio 43952
www.emmausroad.org

∾: ∾

∾: ∾

Library of Congress Control Number: 2008922170
ISBN: 978-1-931018-48-7

∾: ∾

∾: ∾

Cover illustration by R. Genn
Cover design and interior layout by Julie Davis

# DEDICATION

*To Antony Flew, author of* There Is a God: How the World's Most Notorious Atheist Changed His Mind (2007), *for his academic integrity and intellectual fortitude in "following the evidence wherever it may lead..."*

# Acknowledgments

*We are grateful first of all for the loving support of our wives and families.*

*We'd also like to express our gratitude for the benefactors of the St. Paul Center.*

*Finally, our work has benefited immensely from the friendly advice of a non-theist, Phil Goetz who, even though he may not agree with us, has cheerfully caught many errors and pushed us to greater clarity.*

# Contents

Introduction . . . . . . . . . . . . . . . . . . . . . . . . . . . . . . . . 1

Chapter 1: Dawkins' god, Chance . . . . . . . . . . . . . . . . 10

Chapter 2: Pride and Prejudice . . . . . . . . . . . . . . . . . 23

Chapter 3: Dawkins' Fallacious Philosophy . . . . . . . . 52

Chapter 4: Can God's Existence Be Demonstrated? . 75

Chapter 5: The Problem of Morality . . . . . . . . . . . . . 92

Chapter 6: Dawkins' Morality . . . . . . . . . . . . . . . . . . 119

Chapter 7: Dawkins Dismantled . . . . . . . . . . . . . . . . 133

Chapter 8: King Richard . . . . . . . . . . . . . . . . . . . . . . 143

# INTRODUCTION

## Why argue with an Atheist?

We live at a point in history where atheism is shoving its way into the public square, and noisily declaring the need to remove religion. A cadre of militant unbelievers calling themselves The Four Horsemen—Richard Dawkins, Sam Harris, Christopher Hitchens, and Daniel Dennett—have assumed the leadership of a growing Anglo-American movement, releasing volley after volley of bestsellers and DVDs into the Christian culture.

Gone are the days of polite atheism. Christianity is under attack.

What to make of it? In one sense, not much at all. We are reminded of the demon Screwtape's words in C. S. Lewis' brilliant and biting "Screwtape Proposes a Toast." Apologizing to his fellow demons for the meagerness of the fare of souls at the annual dinner of the Tempters' Training College, he remarks "it would be vain to deny that the human souls on whose anguish we have been feasting tonight were of pretty poor quality....Oh, to get one's teeth again into a Farinata, a Henry VIII or even a Hitler!...Instead of this, what do we have tonight?" Mere little sinners but lots of them. "The quality may be wretched," remarks Screwtape to cheer his fellow demons up, "but we never had souls (of a sort) in more abundance."[1] Well, the general quality of the atheists'

1   C. S. Lewis, *The Screwtape Letters, with Screwtape Proposes a Toast* (New York: MacMillan, 1961), 154–155.

arguments now on the market is decidedly low, but "we never had souls (of a sort) in more abundance." Gone are the days of such atheist giants as Friedrich Nietzsche; here are the days of mass-produced unbelief.

Yet there is cause for worry precisely because we live in an age that judges things more by quantity rather than quality. Judging solely in terms of bulk, some might think atheists had won a decisive intellectual victory as if there was a direct correlation between the number of atheist books being hawked in the public square and the number of atheists actually among the public. Even more disturbing, the lack of quality in the atheist fare may all too regrettably be a sign of a corresponding lack of quality in arguments offered by theists, or at least a lack of sufficient intellectual preparation on the part of the audience.

Whatever the cause and despite their quality, the rash of books by atheists has indeed had the effect of bringing some to lose their faith. We offer a personal story from one of us (Scott Hahn), worth telling because it was an important impetus to our writing this book together.

~: :~

One of my normally cheerful colleagues in the theology department at Franciscan University came into my office quite agitated one afternoon this last fall semester. As he reported it, a student had come to him, distressed because several of her fellow theology majors were losing their faith after reading Dawkins' *God Delusion*. My colleague considered the book to be so poorly argued that it was entirely without danger. But what he didn't count on—and what I didn't yet fully comprehend myself—was the power of Dawkins' rhetoric. As a result, they fell entirely under the spell of his words.

Franciscan University of Steubenville is as excellent a faith-filled Catholic college as you'll find. If Dawkins' apology for atheism is creating casualties at Franciscan University, can you imagine what effect it's having at other colleges and universities?

Upon talking over this bad news, Benjamin Wiker and I decided we had to do something. We felt that we have a moral burden of providing sufficient rebuttals to the kinds of arguments that atheists are now offering, especially those of Dawkins, the most popular. We had to write a book, and get it out near the time for the release of the paperback version of *The God Delusion*, an event sure to make Dawkins' book a bestseller twice over.

~: :~

Why not answer every atheist book? It would obviously be too burdensome a task, given that there appears to be no end of new atheist books in sight, to attempt a point-by-point refutation of every one as it appears. Since Dawkins' book is the most influential and the arguments of all the atheists including Dawkins tend to be quite repetitious, we will focus on *The God Delusion* (as supplemented by his other writings). If readers know where Dawkins' flaws are, they will be fairly well-immunized against the other atheists' books as they continue to roll off the presses.

Before leaping into a deeper analysis, we'd like to offer a few words about Dawkins' approach, as well as our own. As our mention of Screwtape implies, Dawkins' *God Delusion* is rather disappointing, and we are not alone in that assessment. Both Christians and atheists, nonscientists and scientists, have panned it. Christian philosopher Alvin Plantinga warns readers that "one shouldn't look to this book for evenhanded and thoughtful commentary. In fact the proportion of insult, ridicule, mockery, spleen, and vitriol is astounding."[2] One of Dawkins' fellow atheists, philosopher and Darwinist advocate Michael Ruse, has said even more harshly, "*The God Delusion* makes me embarrassed to be

---

2  Alvin Plantinga, "The Dawkins Confusion: *Naturalism ad absurdum*," *Books and Culture* (http://www.christianitytoday.com/bc/2007/002/1.21.html).

an atheist..."[3] Christian Terry Eagleton notes sarcastically that "Such is Dawkins's unruffled scientific partiality that in a book of almost four hundred pages, he can scarcely bring himself to concede that a single human benefit has flowed from religious faith, a view which is as a priori improbable as it is false." The problem, Eagleton points out, is that Dawkins is ignorant of the very subject he is so at pains to criticize.[4] Atheist Thomas Nagel notes that since Dawkins aims "to overturn the convention of respect toward religion that belongs to the etiquette of modern civilization," he resorts to "persistently violating the convention, and being as offensive as possible..."[5] Nagel is obviously not in sympathy with Dawkins' crude assaults. Evolutionary geneticist H. Allen Orr states, "Despite my admiration for much of Dawkins's work, I'm afraid that I'm among those scientists who must part company with him here. Indeed, *The God Delusion* seems to me badly flawed. Though I once labeled Dawkins a professional atheist, I'm forced, after reading his new book, to conclude he's actually more an amateur....The most disappointing feature of *The God Delusion* is Dawkins's failure to engage religious thought in any serious way. This is, obviously, an odd thing to say about a book-length investigation of God."[6]

∾ ⁖ ∾

For anyone who has read his other works, *The God Delusion* is a decided letdown. It is caustic and peevish, rather than being genuinely witty or insightful, and has the feel of a book dashed off by someone who is annoyed that his opponents still exist and can barely condescend to dismiss them. As a result, *The God Delusion* is filled with self-con-

---

3 From the cover of Alister McGrath and Joanna McGrath, *The Dawkins Delusion? Atheist Fundamentalism and the Denial of the Divine* (Downers Grove, IL: InterVarsity Press, 2007).

4 Terry Eagleton, "Lunging, Flailing, Mispunching," *London Review of Books* (October 19, 2006).

5 Thomas Nagel, review of *The God Delusion*, "The Fear of Religion," *The New Republic* (10/23/2006): 25–29.

6 H. Allen Orr, "A Mission to Convert," *New York Review of Books*, vol. 54, no. 1 (Jan. 11, 2007).

gratulatory smugness appropriate to gala dinners thrown by people of the same tightly-wound intellectual circle who, after too much wine, trade in spiteful quips about the incomprehensible stupidity of anyone not sharing their opinions.

And Dawkins has no trouble being nasty. A few examples will give the flavor. While he hopes that "religious readers who open it [*The God Delusion*] will be atheists when they put it down," he realizes, of course, that "dyed-in-the-wool faith-heads are immune to argument" because "their resistance [has been] built up over years of childhood indoctrination."[7] Of course, "people of a theological bent are often chronically incapable of distinguishing what is true from what they'd like to be true."[8]

And the spite continues. To the question of whether religion contributes to a more healthy life, Dawkins finds it "hard to believe…that health is improved by the semi-permanent state of morbid guilt suffered by a Roman Catholic possessed of normal human frailty and less than normal intelligence."[9] In regard to the cross-cultural appearance of belief, Dawkins admits that "no known culture lacks some version of the time-consuming, wealth-consuming, hostility-provoking rituals, the anti-factual, counter-productive fantasies of religion."[10] The very title itself belies any hint that Dawkins is seriously engaging those with whom he so passionately disagrees, for a delusion is "a persistent false belief held in the face of strong contradictory evidence," and as Dawkins (borrowing from another author) quips "When one person suffers from delusion, it is called insanity. When many people suffer from a delusion it is called Religion."[11]

---

7    Richard Dawkins, *The God Delusion* (Boston and New York: Houghton Mifflin, 2006), 5.
8    Richard Dawkins, *The God Delusion*, 108.
9    Richard Dawkins, *The God Delusion*, 167.
10   Richard Dawkins, *The God Delusion*, 166.
11   Richard Dawkins, *The God Delusion*, 5.

In addition to the caustic tone, Dawkins has a tendency to slip into logical fallacies and factual errors that are nothing short of astounding. As we point out at several places, he continually assumes what he would have to prove, the fallacy of *petitio principii* or begging the question. Even stranger is his casual treatment of the facts regarding the 20th century's atheistic regimes, which we now know wiped out tens upon tens of millions of lives in the name of unbelief. This leads him to make statements that display a disregard of well-known facts. Given that the Soviet destruction of Orthodox churches is so copiously attested, it is hard to know what to say to someone who could write in all seriousness, "I do not believe there is an atheist in the world who would bulldoze Mecca—or Chartres, York Minster or Notre Dame, the Shwe Dagon, the temples of Kyoto or, of course, the Buddhas of Bamiyan."[12]

We would wish for the kind of philosophical acumen and gracious reasonableness in Dawkins that one finds in Antony Flew, who until quite recently was the world's most famous atheist, the successor of Bertrand Russell and the predecessor of Dawkins himself. For Flew, his "conversion" from atheism to belief in God was rational. "I must say," he states near the end of his last book, *There is a God*, "that the journey to my discovery of the Divine has thus far been a pilgrimage of reason. I have followed the argument where it has led me. And it has led me to accept the existence of a self-existent, immutable, immaterial, omnipotent, and omniscient Being."[13]

This conclusion is anathema to Dawkins. As a consequence, his response to Flew's intellectual conversion was to insinuate that it was a product of senility, and to resort to parody and summary dismissal of the arguments that Flew found persuasive.[14] This follows his general

---

12  Richard Dawkins, *The God Delusion*, 249.
13  Antony Flew, *There Is a God: How the World's Most Notorious Atheist Changed His Mind* (New York: HarperOne, 2007), 155.
14  Richard Dawkins, *The God Delusion*, 82.

pattern. Having neither patience nor sympathy with his opponents renders Dawkins almost completely incapable of presenting the arguments of believers in anything more than an inaccurate caricature.

Ironically, one is reminded in reading Dawkins of the kind of acrimony that is often found among fundamentalist preachers who douse their opponents with scorn and ignite them with rhetoric to create a spectacle of combustion for their audience. The preacher seems thereby to be a true prophet, calling fire down from the heavens to consume the unbelievers in righteous conflagration. Dawkins preaches to his audience in much the same way. Filled with contempt for his opponents, he seems unable to fathom that anyone could rationally disagree with him. Since his opponents must therefore be unreasonable, then they are fit only for a rhetorical scorching that reduces them to pitiable ashes. Over and above all this, just as with the fundamentalist preacher, Dawkins resorts to continual dire, semi-apocalyptic warnings about the impending afflictions that will surely occur if the "mind virus" of religion is not soon cured by atheism—a situation so ominous that it calls for the active intervention by some unnamed official power so that religious indoctrination of children by parents (which Dawkins terms child abuse) can be stopped before humanity's doom is sealed. One feels him to be unknowingly but continually slipping into self-parody.

It might be tempting for believers to respond with equal bitterness and inflamed rhetoric. We think that is as unwise as it is unhelpful. Instead, we shall examine the caliber of Dawkins' statements and arguments on their own merits. As the great Greek philosopher Plato once said, the best way to assess the argumentative core of largely rhetorical speeches, is to strip them of all their rhetoric and analyze the bare arguments. We believe that once this is done, and the caliber of his arguments is gauged, then the very weakness of Dawkins' *God Delusion* will be exposed. That is the main goal of our book.

We must emphasize that our main goal is not to make a case for Christianity or even theism (those interested in these kinds of arguments should read Scott Hahn, *Reasons to Believe*[15]), but to expose the weaknesses of Dawkins' atheism. On his part, Dawkins states that his case against religion is mainly a case against Christianity,[16] and we will assume this as well. But we assume it, for the most part, to assess the caliber of his attack. This means that our defined task is largely negative. Yet, the reader will become aware of a general, natural theological position that emerges from our analysis, and in fact, halfway through this book we do provide a different kind of proof of God's existence after exposing the faults of Dawkins' attempts to disprove the existence of God.

Readers may wonder why we end with faith rather than beginning there. The reason is quite simple. The way to meet an opponent like Dawkins is on *his* ground. If his arguments fail on his own terms, then they are of little use as weapons against the faith. There is another reason to proceed this way, one pointed out by St. Thomas many centuries ago. There is no sense arguing on the basis of Catholic doctrine or Holy Scripture with someone who accepts neither as true.[17] Arguing with an atheist on matters of revelation is an enormous, energy-consuming waste of time. Thus, we lay aside all matters of Divine Revelation, and argue solely on the basis of reason alone.

It is our hope that this book finds its way to those shaken by Dawkins' *God Delusion* so that they may see how shaky his arguments actually are. We shall proceed in a gentlemanly way. If we might borrow from Dawkins, who says before he begins "I shall not go out of my way to offend, but nor shall I don kid gloves to handle religion any more

---

15 Scott Hahn, *Reasons to Believe: How to Understand, Explain, and Defend the Catholic Faith* (New York: Doubleday, 2007), esp. pp. 15–55.

16 Richard Dawkins, *The God Delusion*, 37.

17 St. Thomas Aquinas, *Summa Theologiae*, I.1.8.

gently than I would handle anything else,"[18] we too shall be as gentle as we can be with Dawkins' atheism—but no more. His arguments may seem strong, as long as he can hold forth without an adversary to call his position into question, and we think that he may well realize this.

We offer our book for all those swayed into doubt by Dawkins, so that reason may triumph over rhetoric.

---

18 Richard Dawkins, *The God Delusion*, 27.

# Dawkins' god, Chance

## Statue of Limitations

We're going to begin with an exposure of Richard Dawkins' faith in a particularly strange anti-deity, which for Dawkins functions as his god, the object of his faith, hope, and dare we say, if not love, considerable devotion. If the reader is to understand Dawkins' unwavering confidence in the non-existence of God, he must first of all become acquainted with his irrational faith in "Chance."

What would be the rational reaction to our seeing, in broad daylight, a marble statue of the Virgin Mary suddenly wave at us?

a. Complete astonishment, and overwhelming belief that one had witnessed a miracle.
b. Complete astonishment, and nearly overwhelming belief that one had witnessed a miracle coupled with the conviction that a thorough investigation should be made into another possible cause.
c. Uttering, "That sure was lucky," and going about one's business.

If your response is "a," you would be considered quite normal and rational, but perhaps a bit hasty. If your response is "b," you would be quite normal and rational, but also skeptical enough to allow reason to further investigate. And "c"? You'd be Richard Dawkins—or at least, so it would seem from his arguments.

Why bring up this seemingly absurd scenario? Dawkins brought it up first in a previous bestseller, *The Blind Watchmaker* (and adverts to it once again in his *God Delusion*[1]). While it may be interesting evidence of his irrational belief in the impossibility of miracles, it is hard evidence for his irrational belief in the powers of chance, a belief that has its origins in his intense desire that God not exist.

So let us lay aside for the moment the question of whether miracles do in fact happen. Our concern for now is whether Dawkins' unconquerable faith in the powers of chance is rational. For Dawkins, whatever God could do, chance can do better, and that means that any event, no matter how seemingly miraculous, can be explained as good luck. As we shall see, this directly affects Dawkins' ability to assess the latest scientific evidence that points to the existence of an Intelligent Creator. Before we get to the implications, let's allow Mr. Dawkins' inestimable faith in the powers of chance to speak for itself.

In *The Blind Watchmaker* Dawkins states that "A miracle is something that happens, but which is exceedingly surprising. If a marble statue of the Virgin Mary suddenly waved its hand at us we should treat is as a miracle, because all our experience and knowledge tells us that marble doesn't behave like that." However, he goes on to assure the reader, science would not judge this occurrence as "utterly impossible," but only "very improbable."[2]

This is a fundamental confusion that runs throughout Dawkins, the confusion of improbability with impossibility. "Coincidence," Dawkins assures the reader, "means multiplied improbability." That is

---

1    Richard Dawkins, *The God Delusion*, 373–374.
2    Richard Dawkins, *The Blind Watchmaker: Why the Evidence of Evolution Reveals a Universe without Design* (New York: Norton, 1996), 159.

a fancy way of saying that anything can happen. Since anything is possible, then anything is probable, even if that probability is astronomically small. Back to the waving statue.

> In the case of the marble statue, molecules in solid marble are continuously jostling against one another in random directions. The jostlings of the different molecules cancel one another out, so the whole hand of the statue stays still. But if, by sheer coincidence, all the molecules just happened to move in the same direction at the same moment, the hand would move. If they then all reversed direction at the same moment the hand would move back. In this way it is *possible* for a marble statue to wave at us. It could happen. The odds against such a coincidence are unimaginably great but they are not incalculably great. A physicist colleague has kindly calculated them for me. The number is so large that the entire age of the universe so far is too short a time to write out all the noughts! It is theoretically possible for a cow to jump over the moon with something like the same improbability. The conclusion to this part of the argument is that we can *calculate* our way into regions of miraculous improbability far greater than we can *imagine* as plausible.[3]

We quote this entire paragraph because if we merely reported it, no sane person would believe that Dawkins had written it, or we would be accused of misrepresenting his words or taking them out of context. But there it is, word for word. In stating it this way, Dawkins has gone far beyond the important insight that many things that have an extremely small possibility of happening do have *some* possibility of happening. For some reason, he wants his reader to assume that the impossible is really only extremely improbable.

3   Richard Dawkins, *The Blind Watchmaker*, 159–160.

The first, most obvious objection to this kind of reasoning is this: What *would* be impossible if *anything*—or at least any physical event of the kind described—is possible? And if such impossible things are possible, why isn't it possible that the waving statue was indeed a miraculous occurrence? Why isn't the miraculous itself a possibility?

The answer is quite simple. Dawkins believes that *anything but a miracle is possible*, and that leads him to believe that the impossible, no matter how absurd, is possible. The moon, over which the cow really could jump, truly might—just for a few moments, due to random molecular restructuring—be made of green cheese.

This leads to a second point. Quite obviously, Dawkins' presentation of the miraculous and impossible is only a manifestation of his atheism. What kind of an atheist is he? In his *God Delusion*, Dawkins classifies himself as a *de facto* atheist ("I cannot know for certain but I think God is very improbable, and I live my life on the assumption that he is not there"[4]). He adds that "I am agnostic only to the extent that I am agnostic about fairies at the bottom of the garden."[5]

But here is the problem. Since he has reclassified impossible things to be only highly improbable, it is unclear what the difference would be in his assessment of (1) a waving Virgin Mary statue, (2) a cow suddenly jumping approximately 240,000 miles in the air, calculating its ascent so as to take into account the effect of the earth's rotation and the drag of the atmosphere (and somehow avoiding combustion by atmospheric friction), (3) fairies at the bottom of the garden, and (4) the existence of God. In short, if God is only highly improbable, could His existence be any *less* probable than an event of such mind-numbing improbability that one couldn't write down the calculated improbability in 13 ½ billion years? Given the outrageous-

---

4   Richard Dawkins, *The God Delusion*, 51.
5   Richard Dawkins, *The God Delusion*, 51.

ly enormous improbability, how could one even calculate accurately *which* was more probable? If on Dawkins' reckoning God is at least as probable as the sudden waving of a marble statue, then according to his own reasoning God causing the miraculous waving of the Virgin Mary statue is at least as probable as random atomic jostling.

We also might well ask at this point what it means to say that the existence of God is probable. Dawkins gives only this thin explanation: "reason alone could not propel one to total conviction that anything definitely does not exist."[6] Whatever the merits or intention of this proviso, we would like to propose a correction that will come into play when we examine Dawkins' attempts at demonstrations that allegedly propel one to almost total conviction that God does not exist. Simply put, God's existence is not a matter of probability. Either He does exist or He doesn't exist. Things that enter the realm of probability are contingent; they are the *kind* of things that don't necessarily have to be. By contrast, God is eternal by definition; by definition, if He exists, He exists of necessity outside of time.

We say "if He exists" and "by definition" so that this distinction doesn't depend at this point on our actually having proven that God does exist, and we also want to make clear that we are not, like St. Anselm, permitting a proof of God's existence by definition. We can have a definition of something that doesn't exist, like a horned horse. But having a horn and being a horse must of *necessity* go together when we are examining the question of whether a unicorn exists, in much the same way that having eternal existence and being God go together when we are examining the question of whether or not God exists. We cannot ask, "What is the probability that God exists?" for the same reason we cannot ask, "What is the probability that a unicorn has a horn in the middle of its forehead?"

---

6   Richard Dawkins, *The God Delusion*, 51.

We submit, then, that God's existence isn't probable. But again, saying that doesn't decide the case for God. We would still have to demonstrate that a necessary Being, God, does in fact exist. Probability does enter in, but only with regard to our arguments falling short of being entirely demonstrable. We may have probable arguments for His necessary existence or against it, in the same way that we can have probable arguments about the current existence of liquid water on a certain planet outside our solar system. In both cases, the fact exists—either God does or doesn't exist; either there is or is not liquid water—and the probability has to do with the type and caliber of *our* arguments given what we happen to know at the point we make them. We'll come back to this point.

For now, let's return to Dawkins' seemingly limitless faith in chance. Given what we've said, we would like to offer a reformulation of famed atheist philosopher David Hume's maxim in regard to the miraculous:[7] *No event that is more miraculous than the miracle that it seeks to discredit can be used as an explanation to deny that a miracle actually occurred.* To any sane person who witnessed a marble statue of the Virgin Mary waving to him (and who then eliminated all possibility of there being some kind of trickery, illusion, or delusion), the possibility that it was indeed miraculous would be less miraculous than the possibility that it was the result of randomly synchronized subatomic jostling.

We'll find our maxim very handy when we turn to Dawkins' attempt to convince readers of the materialistic miracle of life's origin—for that is the real goal of all his talk about miracles. Before doing this,

---

7   Hume's maxim is as follows: "No testimony is sufficient to establish a miracle, unless the testimony be of such a kind, that its falsehood would be more miraculous, than the fact, which it endeavours to establish." David Hume, *An Enquiry Concerning Human Understanding* (Indianapolis, IN: Hackett, 1981), chap. 10, p. 77. In setting out this maxim, Hume was trying to set forth a final refutation of the miraculous in Scripture. Since the miracles in Scripture are only reported to us by other alleged witnesses—that is, we didn't witness them ourselves—then it is far more likely that the alleged witnesses were liars or fools.

however, we need to make even more clear the difference between the impossible and the improbable, a distinction of which Dawkins seems to have lost sight. Here is a simple illustration in the form of two questions.

1.  What is the probability of "a perfect deal in bridge, where each of the four players receives a complete suite of cards"[8]?
2.  What is the probability of throwing a deck of cards up in the air during a hurricane and having the cards land as a four-story card house, where each story is made up of a "complete suite of cards"?

We can calculate the first, and Dawkins has done it: "The odds against this happening are 2,235,197,406,895,366,368,301,559,999 to 1."[9] And the card house in the hurricane? The odds against it happening aren't really big; or even really, really big. There are no odds at all. It can't happen. It is physically impossible—just like random jostling of a statue's marble hands or cows jumping over the moon. This is a different kind of impossibility, than the impossibility of dealing a poker hand of five aces with a standard deck where there are only four (unless, to be tiresome, we allow the Dawkinsian possibility of the atomic reconfiguration of a joker into another ace).

What do we learn from this about Dawkins' argument? Again, a sign of the weakness of Dawkins' position is that he is forced to treat the impossible as possible so that he can eliminate any possibility of the miraculous (which is the only thing that he rules out, *a priori*, as impossible). "My thesis," he tells readers, is "that events that we commonly call miracles are not supernatural, but are part of a spectrum of more-or-less improbable natural events. A miracle, in other words, if it occurs at

---

8   An example used by Dawkins himself, so we can't be accused of stacking the deck. *The Blind Watchmaker*, 161.
9   Richard Dawkins, *The Blind Watchmaker*, 161.

all, is a tremendous stroke of luck. Events don't fall neatly into natural events *versus* miracles....Given infinite time, or infinite opportunities, anything is possible."[10] Anything but the miraculous, that is.

Strictly speaking, however, a miracle *is* possible for Dawkins, but it just cannot really be miraculous. Jesus Christ rising from the dead is possible in just exactly the same way that random jostlings of marble molecules could make a statue wave or a cow jump over the moon. In fact, *all* the miracles in the Old and New Testaments could actually have happened just as reported, the only difference being that they were highly improbable molecular events.

Of course, we do not mean that Dawkins himself *really* thinks that everything, no matter how loony or absurd or "miraculous," is possible. Rather, he is using this type of argument for a purpose. He uses his unbounded faith in chance as a means to establish purely materialistic explanations for events that would seem to any sane person to require a supernatural cause.

To be more pointed, Dawkins manifests a *selective* confusion of the possible and the impossible when it suits his purposes, and sometimes the confusion amounts to an intellectual slight-of-hand that has fooled many of Dawkins' readers (and, we assume, even Dawkins himself). Let's look at a particularly interesting example from his *God Delusion* about the "miracle" of life's appearance on earth, for this is how Dawkins purports to show that a Creator God is unnecessary.

According to Dawkins, we can safely estimate that there are, somewhere in the vast universe, a "billion billion" planets that would be suitable for life. He then supposes what he takes to be long odds of one in a billion of life arising by chance (although he really doesn't mean life, but merely "the spontaneous arising of something equivalent to DNA.") Well, then, concludes Dawkins, "even with such absurdly long odds, *life*

---

10 Richard Dawkins, *The Blind Watchmaker*, 139.

*will still have arisen on a billion planets—of which Earth, of course, is one."* This is such a surprising conclusion, Dawkins remarks, "I'll say it again. If the odds of life originating spontaneously on a planet were a billion to one against, nevertheless that stupefyingly improbable event would still happen on a billion planets."[11]

It is such a surprising conclusion precisely because it doesn't follow. The entire argument is faulty. We'll get to more particular questions in regard to physics and chemistry in the next chapter but, at this point, we call attention to a problem in Dawkins' reasoning that is a matter of logic. You cannot assume what you have to prove; that is called "begging the question" or more elegantly, the fallacy of *petitio principii*. He falls into the fallacy because he assumes without argument that the spontaneous assembly of DNA is like getting a perfect deal in bridge rather than being like tossing a perfect cardhouse in a hurricane. That is what he would have to *prove* rather than assume.

The real question, the prior question, is one of possibility and impossibility, not greater or lesser probability. If tossing a perfect cardhouse in a hurricane is impossible because the cards would keep blowing away, then it wouldn't become possible by adding into the calculation a billion billion available planets, or even a trillion trillion. If the spontaneous arising of DNA is simply impossible, then it wouldn't matter how many billions or trillions of planets there were. It couldn't and wouldn't happen. Thus, we have to be very wary that Dawkins is not assuming that what is impossible is just very, very unlikely.

Even admitting the possibility of "the spontaneous arising of something equivalent to DNA," it is grossly misleading merely to assume such an easy probability as a billion to one. If the odds were really that good, then there wouldn't be significant skepticism among scientists about origin of life scenarios. We'll see in the next chap-

---

11 Richard Dawkins, *The God Delusion*, 137–138. Emphasis added.

ter why that skepticism is well-founded. But for now, we can at least note that it wouldn't take much to worsen the odds so that Dawkins' "proof" would fail. That is because of the way probabilities "grow." The probability of rolling a five with a normal six-sided die is one in six. But the probability of rolling two fives in a row is $\frac{1}{6}$ x $\frac{1}{6}$ or one in thirty-six. Ten in a row: one in 60,466,176. Twenty in a row: one in 3,656,158,440,062,976. Twenty-five in a row: one in 28,430,288, 029,929,701,376. It doesn't take long to climb above one in a billion odds, nor even to climb above one in a billion billion odds. As a consequence, the introduction of even a relatively small number of adverse factors would affect Dawkins' generous assignation of a billion and one odds of the spontaneous production of DNA and soon enough eliminate his easy-going conclusion that "life will still have arisen on a billion planets—of which Earth, of course, is one." And so, we cannot allow ourselves to think that Dawkins can settle the question merely by assigning a billion to one odds. He must first show that it is possible and then give a reasonable conjecture in regard to the odds.

Of course, that is a matter of scientific detail. Before we do enter into the scientific details in the next chapter, let us close with several observations. We think it is fair to say that Dawkins' faith in the powers of chance is at least as strong, if not stronger, than most people's faith in God. We are justified in calling it faith for two reasons. First, Dawkins himself admits that the existence of God "is very improbable," rather than absolutely, demonstrably impossible. We assume that he is not agnostic about the existence of a four-angled triangle.

Clearly, Dawkins would not appreciate our categorizing his *de facto* atheism as a kind of faith. "Atheists do not have faith," he assures the reader; it is just that "reason alone could not propel one to total conviction that anything definitely does not exist."[12] But if not reason alone,

---

12 Richard Dawkins, *The God Delusion*, 51.

then reason and what? Is he not saying "I *believe* God does not exist even though by reason alone I cannot demonstrate it"?

Obviously Dawkins intends to dodge this by asserting that reason by its very nature cannot "propel one to total conviction that anything definitely does not exist." As he notes, on such grounds, the existence of fairies at the bottom of the garden cannot be definitely disproved.

Does that seem rational? What propels Dawkins to allow for this absurdity? Precisely his desire to demonstrate to the reader that God does not exist—a bit of a paradox, to say the least. Because Dawkins wants to affirm that the miraculous does not require a supernatural cause, he is willing to affirm that *anything* is possible so as to allow that chance can provide a materialist explanation of any apparent miracle, such as a waving Virgin Mary statue or the "spontaneous arising" of something equivalent to DNA on Earth. In that way, he can dispense with a God who performs miracles and a Creator God in one fell blow. But since *anything* is possible, then "reason alone could not propel one to total conviction that anything definitely does not exist."

An interesting trap, isn't it? The desire to eliminate God brings Dawkins to embrace an absurdity—that anything can happen. But having thrown himself into absurdity's embrace, he finds that he cannot entirely eliminate God, the very thing that brought him to leap into the arms of absurdity. At least he is consistent, but this consistency leads him to the position of agnosticism that makes his unbelief a kind of faith.

This brings us to a second reason we may call Dawkins' agnosticism faith. It would be harder to imagine a more fervent faith in the powers of chance than someone who can, with a straight face, speak of the actual possibility of a marble statue waving its hand or a cow jumping over the moon. Such "miraculous improbability" is indistinguishable from the early Christian Tertullian's famous statement of faith (from *De carne Christi*) in regard to the resurrection of Jesus Christ that *certum est, quia impossibile* (it is certain, because it is impossible). (Tertullian did not say, as it is often reported, *credo quia absurdum est*, "I believe because it is absurd.") The point of what Tertullian did say was that since the resurrection was an impossible event, it must (as faith maintains) have been a miraculous event. Dawkins changes Tertullian's statement of faith only to the extent that he believes that an impossible event is certain because it is miraculously improbable. But that is not much different, is it, than the alleged saying of Tertullian, *credo quia absurdum est*? Why such devotion to the great and fickle god, Chance? Quite simple. He would rather believe in *anything* but God.

But who is this god Chance? How can it be such a powerful cause, so powerful that it can replace the need for a living, acting, intelligent Creator God? As Aristotle long ago pointed out to the materialists of his day—who likewise worshiped at the altar of Chance—chance isn't really a cause because it really isn't a thing. There is the chance *of* something happening, but the "of" is all important because that tells you what really exists and defines what you can possibly mean by chance. Yet, even here, chance isn't a thing.

To use a familiar example, there is a one-in-six chance of rolling a five on a six-sided die, but here "chance" isn't a thing or a cause. What causes the one-in-six chance is the fact that there exists in reality a six-sided die that it is made in such a way that it can be rolled, it can stop rolling, and so on. Thus, a 1/6 chance isn't a thing in addition to the die, but a short-hand way of describing the actual entities and conditions that allow for six different but roughly equal possibilities of some very particular well-defined event to occur. We can eliminate the 1/6 chance by changing the die or the conditions, say, by filing off the dots of the die or throwing the die into a blast furnace. That cuts the great god Chance down to size, making it not a powerful and primary cause, but a secondary shadow of other beings and causes. Dawkins himself actually understands this point quite clearly in regard to natural selection. As he remarks in many places, natural selection (insofar as it is a cumulative, step-by-step building up of favorable traits) is the "opposite" of chance. His point is this. If natural selection had to produce an eye in one, giant random set of mutations, we really would be making evolution entirely a matter of chance, and hence next to impossible, because the material parts (the various atoms) have no tendency to spontaneously take on multi-layered, super-complex biological structure. We would be relying on chance to do what only a god could do. But evolution builds the eye by tiny steps, each of which involves only a slight bit of chance acting according to the normal mutation rates in genes. Here, chance is not some kind of miracle-performing god, but something that is understandable in terms of and subordinate to what genes are, how they copy, and what can effect the genetic text of a DNA molecule.

But as we've seen, chance grows to monstrous proportions when Dawkins attempts to explain why *anything* can happen. The reason, as we have seen, is that Dawkins wants to use chance to replace God in regard to the origin of life. Since it must have the powers of the God it displaces, then it grows accordingly, becoming a god that can do anything. Of course, Dawkins doesn't need his god to do everything, but only those things that he surmises natural selection cannot do, and that would seem to require a real God to do: create the first living things. Let us now see how well this god can do.

# 2

# Pride and Prejudice

What does it take to beat billion-to-one odds?

In the last chapter we have witnessed Dawkins' nearly unfathomable faith in chance. We submit that this faith distorts his judgment of the most important scientific issues and questions that pertain to the existence of God. Dawkins would rather believe in *anything* than be induced by reason to admit that there is a good scientific case to be made for the existence of an intelligent cause of nature. He will grasp at any materialist miracle, as long as it is not a real spiritual miracle. But in doing so, as we shall see, he violates our quite reasonable maxim: *No event that is more miraculous than the miracle that it seeks to discredit can be used as an explanation to deny that a miracle actually occurred.*

Dawkins' main area of expertise is evolutionary biology, and he believes that natural selection can do *anything* once it gets going, that is, once there is in place some kind of a living being, no matter how simple, that can copy and pass on its storehouse of DNA. "Once the vital ingredient—some kind of genetic molecule—is in place, true Darwinian natural selection can follow, and complex life emerges as the eventual consequence."[1] Whether such unblinking confidence in the powers of Darwinian natural selection is warranted or not, we may leave to the side at this point.

---

1   Richard Dawkins, *The God Delusion*, 137.

First things first. Even Dawkins admits that getting to the point where evolution can take off is no easy matter. How far back before evolution do we need to go? For the sake of following out his argument, we need to go to the beginning of the universe. Before there was ever biology, there was only chemistry. That is, if we trace backwards the history of Earth as it fits into science's current account of the history of the universe, we find the first very simple cells arising on Earth some 3.7 billion years ago, the Earth itself forming some 4.5 billion years ago, and the universe coming into existence about 13.5 billion years ago. What was the universe doing for 10 billion years before the first living cells arose on Earth?

Preparing for life. Complex biology—and even the simplest living cell is extraordinarily complex—takes a lot of complex chemistry. The needed chemical elements that make up all biological structures didn't just pop into existence; they were literally cooked-up in the furnaces of successive generations of stars, over billions of years. In fact, it took about half the age of the universe to beget a rich enough diversity of chemical elements to build even the simplest living cell. But, of course, merely having the needed elements doesn't mean a cell automatically pops into existence, any more than having a load of bricks, lumber, glass, and shingles results in them leaping together to automatically create a house. *A necessary condition is not a sufficient condition.*

Before delving into the problem of how the first cell came to be, we must note that it is actually a problem for atheists that the chemical elements themselves did not always exist, and that the universe itself had a beginning rather than being eternal. If the universe had been around forever, stocked with the full array of 100-plus chemical elements we find neatly stacked on our Periodic Table of Elements, then it would seem that just by the chance jostling around of elements, somewhere, sometime, you would be bound to get a lucky combination. Forever is, to say the least, a rather long time. It boggles the mind, and makes anything seem possible.

But the fact that the universe had a very definite beginning, as did the chemical elements, creates severe difficulties on several different levels for anyone, including Dawkins, who wants to displace God with chance. To begin with, while God can create instantaneously or over any period of time He wishes, chance needs a long, long, long time to accomplish even the most meager results. The reason for this is that intelligent beings can choose intelligently. Chance is the complete absence of intelligence, choice, and, we should add, causal power.

We can illustrate this point by recalling Dawkins' example of "a perfect deal in bridge, where each of the four players receives a complete suite of cards." If we wanted to make sure that we dealt a perfect deal on the very first try, we could easily "stack the deck," that is, choose to set up the cards intelligently in advance. But if we wanted to leave it up to chance—that is, without the intervention of our intelligent choice—we'd shuffle the cards, and see how long it would take to get a perfect deal. (Actually, if we *really* wanted to leave it up to pure chance, we would simply let the deck sit there in hopes that the wind or other accidental causes might shuffle and deal the cards.) The problem is, as Dawkins rightly stated, that the "odds against this happening are 2,235,197,406,895,366,368,301,559,999 to 1."

What does that staggering improbability mean in terms of *time?* Well, there are only 31,570,560 seconds in a year, so as it turns out, the universe has been around for only 426,202,560,000,000,000 seconds. If a computer could somehow deal out all the possible combinations of cards to four people at one deal per second, it would take well over 5 billion times the age of the universe to go through every possibility. Of course, it *could* happen on the very first try (or the second or third), but the odds are astronomically against it. Furthermore, unlike the machine which does not duplicate non-perfect hands but methodically and efficiently plows through all combinations without repetition, a real human dealer would repeat any of the enormous number of imperfect hands, rather than work his way to the perfect hand by methodically eliminating the imperfect. Furthermore, each physical shuffling and dealing would take considerably longer than one second. A real dealer would almost surely die before dealing a perfect hand in bridge. We mention this important point because nature works more like a real dealer, than an obsessively methodical machine.

Now if the universe existed forever, well then, time's not a problem. You've got more than enough time to spare. But setting a definite beginning point to the universe creates an enormous difficulty for the godless workings of chance. You haven't got forever; you've only got 13½ billion years. Actually, as it turns out, since our focus is on the possibility of random chemical combinations on Earth, then we've only got 4½ billion years. Even more daunting, since the Earth wasn't cool enough for living things until about 3.8 billion years ago, we've got even less time.

Well, what actually happened? Against all odds, the simplest cell formed on our planet *almost immediately* upon our planet being cool enough to allow for the simplest biological life. If getting the right chemical combination to allow for the simplest cell by chance is anything like getting a perfect deal in bridge, we are (if we take Dawkins' view of things) really, really, really lucky. It looks like somebody stacked the deck.

That is obviously not the conclusion he wants to draw. Rather than allowing a deck-stacker, Dawkins wants to be an odds-stacker. We've seen that Dawkins gets around the overwhelming-odds problem by the blank declaration that the chance of the rise of something like DNA is about a billion to one—and even declares that he does "not for a moment believe the origin of life was anywhere near so improbable in practice."[2] He believes the odds were *even better* than a billion to one. Believing the odds to be that good allows him to avoid inferring a divine deck-stacker.

The difficulty is this: we are not aware of very many competent biologists, physicists, or chemists who share Dawkins' jaunty optimism about the possibilities for the chance production of DNA, let alone the cell in which it could function. Why is Dawkins' confidence so rare among scientists who deal with origin of life questions?

As we mentioned, even the simplest cell is very complex. For Dawkins' purposes, he's quite willing to strip away most of the complexity of an actual cell, and consider it as basically a piece of DNA (which is a little like stripping away the actual complexity of a factory and considering just its architectural blueprints). He does this because he's an evolutionary biologist, and one of a particular stripe: as he makes clear in his *Selfish Gene*, everything is reducible to the genetic information on the DNA strand in the cell. Once you've got that, everything else follows. Let's grant him this erroneous reductionism for a minute. Does his optimism stand up?

DNA is a nucleic acid that stores the cell's genetic information in the form of a strand, consisting of sequences of the nitrogenous bases A, G, C, T (abbreviations for adenine, guanine, cytosine, and thymine). Even for a very, very small DNA strand of 100 bases—much, much smaller than we find in any actual cell—the odds against getting a particular lucky combination is staggering, $4^{100}$ to one against. We can *see* the difference quite clearly between the actual probability and Dawkins' super-optimistic odds. Dawkins believes that the odds against a propitious string of DNA arising by chance are 1,000,000,000 to one. But when we do the actual calculations we find that the odds against it are a bit over 1,600,000,000,000,000,000,000,000,000,000,000,000,

---

2   Richard Dawkins, *The God Delusion*, 138.

000,000,000,000,000,000,000 to one. You don't have to be either a scientist or a statistician to see the difference in the number of zeroes.

Of course, we can't simply compare the two. Dawkins was asserting the odds in regard to DNA arising on one planet in a billion (without disclosing anything about how those odds were calculated or estimated) over a time period of some millions of years on each planet, not the odds of getting a particular DNA strand in one fell swoop. It is possible to whittle down the atrocious $4^{100}$ odds by multiplying the number of trials, the length of time, and the sheer bulk of chemical sub-components that are jostling about. (As a parallel, imagine the effect of adding 10,000,000 dealers all working for 10,000,000 years so as to cut down the odds that only *one* of them would deal a perfect deal in bridge.) If we add enough such factors, it would seem we could eventually approach Dawkins' optimistic billion to one odds.

The difficulty, however, is that conditions could easily be added that would drive things back again in the other direction, right back up to $4^{100}$ against, and these are the very factors that make scientists wary of assuming easy odds. The nitrogenous bases—A, G, C, T—aren't themselves just going to leap into being and start jostling around. They have to be built up, bit by bit, and one would have to calculate the probabilities of chemicals randomly associating step by step. This is difficult, to say the least. In attempting it, we should not confuse laboratory conditions with natural conditions. In the lab, scientists can begin each step with a high concentration of the necessary chemical materials. In nature, the result of each step would be an almost inconsequentially small amount of the chemical needed for the next step. If we might illustrate the difficulty, imagine the probability of a billion to one of getting complex chemical B randomly from simpler chemical materials (which, for convenience, we can collectively call A). Success means that a billion "trials" yields *one* positive result. That's not very much to go on, and in fact reduces the odds drastically of randomly climbing from B to C. Obviously we may multiply the number of trials, but that contains the hidden problem of accounting for a far greater concentration of A. How did *that* arise? So we are back at this basic insight. Under natural conditions, we can always expect that the amount of the desired chemical that has been produced for the next step will be quite small (otherwise, its production wouldn't have been a matter of small odds), and therefore, each step begins with a dilute amount of the needed chemicals that will be randomly associating for the next step, thereby driving up the odds against success in gaining the next level of chemical complexity. Pictures of oceans densely-packed with nucleic or amino acids are fantasy rather than fact.

Furthermore, since each chemical step arises under peculiar conditions, the possibility of having these conditions at the right time must also be factored in. It is not just a matter of figuring abstract, mathematical odds, or as simple as getting a winning combination. Even supposing a significant number of winning combinations, a great many of them would simply be washed away and unused.

But as it turns out, the very notion of getting something like DNA has little point. If we cast away Dawkins' reductionism, and enter the real world of the cell, we realize that DNA is only a *part* of a living cell. Even granting the absurdity of DNA's jostling into existence, the cell is much more than DNA. While DNA stores information that the cell uses to perform its ongoing complex functions, it is the cell itself that reads DNA and translates it into the structure and activity of life. Without the cell, the DNA is functionless, which means that its information is meaningless. It is a language for which there is no reader, a blueprint without a builder.

What that means can be understood by illustration. Envision coming upon a piece of paper with the following sentence. "In most cases, you will not need to use a pause. You can store up to 32 digits and the pause function counts as 1 of these digits." That is a functional instruction proportionate to a DNA strand of 100 bases. But instruction for *what?* There is no context to tell us. The information is meaningless until we realize that it is part of a telephone's operating instructions. Of course, we know what a telephone is because they now exist, but imagine this snippet of instruction arriving by some magical means a thousand years before the invention of the telephone. What can it mean to anyone? That, in an analogous way, is what it is like to have a DNA sequence show up before a cell.

And so, for DNA to exist as information, there must be a cell in which it can function as information. But here's the catch. The cell isn't made of DNA. The cell itself is made of proteins (and proteins of amino acids), and it is the vast array of protein structures and protein-based activities that allow the genetic code of DNA to "come to life."

So now we would need the chance generation of a multitude of protein structures as well as DNA. Here, the same problem arises as with DNA itself. Proteins are made of amino acids that (like the nitrogenous bases of DNA) must occur in very particular sequences. Choosing again even a very small protein with only 100 amino acids, we find that the probability of getting the right combination by chance is far, far beyond Dawkins billion to one. The odds are actually $20^{100}$ to one, against. Dawkins throws out the easy odds of 1,000,000,000 to one. But when we do the actual calculations using only a very modest protein, we find the odds at about 12,000,000,000,000,000,000,000,000,000,000, 000,000,000,000,000,000,000,000,000,000,000,000,000,000,000, 000,000,000,000,000,000,000,000,000,000,000,000,000,000,000, 000,000,000,000 to one against getting the simplest protein structure by chance. Again, you don't have to be either a scientist or a statistician to see the difference in the number of zeroes.

Since you can't run a cell with a single dinky protein strand (any more than a single dinky DNA strand), that means the probability against the chance rise of enough proteins to make even the simplest functional cell is compounded beyond all calculation. As with nucleic acids and DNA, so also with proteins. There are ways to cut down these odds, but once again, we have to add back in the same kind of factors that drove up the improbability in the case of DNA. Yet, even this may not matter anyway precisely because the protein structures of the cell cannot replicate themselves without DNA. Thus, we are faced with what in origin of life studies is called the chicken and the egg problem. A cell needs both DNA and protein to function; getting them both and getting them integrated stretches the bounds of probability to the breaking point.

If the odds are this bad—so bad that they amount to the closest thing next to impossible that's possible—what could account for Dawkins' incalculable faith in chance? To begin with, he thinks he's got nothing to prove: "however improbable the origin of life might be," Dawkins assures the reader, "we know it happened on Earth because we are here."[3]

*That* is not an argument. It is, at best, an assumption dressed up as a demonstration. One could just as well demonstrate that fairies create life, for "we know it happened on Earth because we are here." Again, we have the fallacy of a *petitio principii*: it proves nothing because it proves anything.

Boiling down his presentation, it amounts to something like this (if we might borrow from his own grating caricature of a theist in *The God Delusion*[4]):

---

3  Richard Dawkins, *The God Delusion*, 137.
4  Richard Dawkins, *The God Delusion*, 80.

"Bet you I can prove life arose by chance."

"What? Go ahead!"

"However improbable the origin of life might be, we know it happened on Earth because we are here. There! You don't need God! So I've proved that God does not exist. Nur Nurny Nur Nur. All theists are fools."

It should be obvious that there is something very fishy about assuming what you would have to prove. Earth is the only place that we know of where any life exists. You can't just assume that life occurred on Earth by chance *because* you know that life happens to exist on Earth. You don't *know* life exists on Earth by chance; *that* is what needs proving. As we've seen above, such a demonstration would have to overcome nearly incalculable odds (or, at least far, far greater than what Dawkins has assumed in asserting that DNA would arise on a billion planets out of a billion billion).

Since we don't simply want to accuse him of rhetorical swindling, how could Dawkins make such an obvious mistake? His mistake is rooted, in part, in his misunderstanding of something called the "anthropic principle." The anthropic principle arose in the latter part of the twentieth century for two related reasons: (1) the discovery that the universe has a definite beginning and (2) the discovery that the beginning had to be very precisely "tuned" or we wouldn't be here. Let's explain a bit more, using the generally-accepted account of the Big Bang.

The Big Bang didn't have to result in making a universe at all, or at least not one that would allow for life. If, for example, there were just a bit more initial energy (or just a little less matter), the Big Bang would have resulted in cosmic confetti. The universe would expand with such force that no stars could form. But stars are where the chemical elements are formed, and without a vast medley of different chemical elements—hydrogen, oxygen, nitrogen, carbon, and so on—there would be no chemical building blocks of life. No stars; no chemical elements; no planets; no life. Shift a little in the other direction and begin with a little less energy (or a little more matter), and gravity would turn the explosion heaving back onto itself in a massive, lifeless crunch.

Change the fundamental forces of nature just a tad—the strong nuclear force, the weak force, gravity, and electromagnetism—and you've got other problems. For example, atoms have protons in their nuclei. If you lighten up the strong force that holds them together just a bit, then you'd have a universe consisting only of hydrogen; that is, a lifeless universe. Increase the electromagnetic force, and you've got just about the same thing.

We know that all life is carbon-based and that oxygen is the stuff of life. But as it turns out, the universe's production of these two essential elements in the supply demanded by life takes absolutely extraordinary fine-tuning, so extraordinary that physicist and agnostic Fred Hoyle famously stated that "A commonsense interpretation of the facts suggests that a super intellect has monkeyed with physics, as well as chemistry and biology, and that there are no blind forces worth speaking about in nature."[5]

Thus, at the very beginning of the universe we find that the universe didn't just go "bang" as the unfortunate name "Big Bang" implies. Explosions aren't finely calibrated events. As scientific research has revealed over the last quarter century, in one instance after another, the Big Bang would have to have been an astonishingly fine-tuned event. But fine-tuning doesn't stop there. Layers of precise calibration go all the way forward to the very exacting conditions that allow for com-

---

5    Quoted in Paul Davies, *The Accidental Universe* (Cambridge: Cambridge University Press, 1982), 118. Hoyle's famous quote comes from an unpublished University of Cardiff preprint entitled, "The Universe: Some Past and Present Reflections."

plex life to exist on Earth. We have provided only a few of the many examples.[6] But even if we focus only on the beginning of the universe, the precision is so stunning as to be incalculable, so that physicists like Michael Turner have resorted to analogy: "The precision," he says, "is as if one could throw a dart across the entire universe and hit a bullseye one millimeter in diameter on the other side."[7]

We've now got the basics of the anthropic principle, which certainly *looks* like it demands a Divine explanation. The key to its being called "anthropic" is simply this: without all this fine-tuning that runs all the way from the origin of the universe to the precise conditions that allow for life on Earth, we human beings (*anthrōpos* is Greek for human being) wouldn't be here. The universe can't just be any old way; the way of life is astoundingly demanding in its exact requirements. Brandon Carter, who coined the term, put it forth in the barest possible form: "What we can expect to observe [as scientists] must be restricted by the conditions necessary for our presence as observers."[8] If we might flesh it out somewhat, human existence demands certain quite definite conditions that extend all the way back to the very beginning of the universe. It is impossible to have complex biological creatures who engage in science [i.e., as observers of the universe] unless these conditions are met; therefore, since there *are* scientists who

6   For a more thorough discussion, readers may consult Martin Rees, *Just Six Numbers: The Deep Forces that Shape the Universe* (New York: Basic Books, 2000); Peter Ward and Donald Brownlee, *Rare Earth: Why Complex Life is Uncommon in the Universe* (New York: Copernicus, 2000); Guillermo Gonzalez and Jay Richards, *The Privileged Planet: How Our Place in the Cosmos Is Designed for Discovery* (Washington, DC: Regnery, 2004); Benjamin Wiker and Jonathan Witt, *A Meaningful World: How the Arts and Sciences Reveal the Genius of Nature* (Downers Grove, IL: InterVarsity Press, 2006), chaps. 6–7; Paul Davies, *Cosmic Jackpot: Why Our Universe Is Just Right for Life* (Boston and New York: Houghton Mifflin Company, 2007), chap. 7.

7   Quoted in Gerald Schroeder, *The Science of God* (New York: Broadway Books, 1997), 5.

8   Brandon Carter, "Large Number Coincidences and the Anthropic Principle in Cosmology," introduction to *Confrontation of Cosmological Theories with Observational Data*, edited by M. S. Longair (Dordrecht: Reidel, 1974), 291–298.

*are in fact observing* the universe, we can expect to find that we live in a universe where these fine-tuned conditions have been met; otherwise, to state the obvious, we wouldn't be here.

Please note! Carter was only stating the obvious. He was not explaining how the universe came to be precisely calibrated. He was only pointing out that we know it has been precisely calibrated otherwise we wouldn't be here. He was stating *at most* that human life is an extremely improbable event, not that either God or chance was the cause. In fact, he said nothing at all about the ultimate cause.

Of course, since the extraordinary fine-tuning is exactly the kind of thing we would expect of an Intelligent Being—or to get at it from the other end, since extraordinary fine-tuning is precisely what we wouldn't expect from blind chance—it is much more likely that it occurred through God rather than chance. The reason, again, is that it is so fine-tuned, that the probability of it happening by chance is astronomically small. The fine-tuning is the focus of the anthropic principle; the calculations of probability only serve to illustrate *how* fine-tuned. If you witnessed the "fine-tuned" arrangement of stone, wood, glass, and open space in a cathedral you could calculate the odds of it happening by chance, but that would be to illuminate how precisely calibrated the cathedral was, not that it in fact came about by chance. That is why the anthropic principle has led many scientists and philosophers to theistic conclusions.

But Dawkins could never accept such theistic implications. Instead, he tries to wriggle free by entirely confusing what the anthropic principle actually says, changing it into a *proof* that the nearly incalculably improbable event was indeed caused by chance (focusing on what is secondary in the anthropic principle). This allows him to set the anthropic principle (so misunderstood) as an *alternative* and *opposite* hypothesis to divine design: "there are two hypotheses to explain what happened—the design hypothesis and the scientific or 'anthropic' hypothesis."[9] Herein lies the confusion. Properly speaking, the original anthropic principle, by implication, set up two alternative and opposite hypotheses to explain fine-tuning: intelligent design and chance. The anthropic principle itself cannot *be* an alternative; it is what makes two other alternatives possible.

Treating the anthropic principle as an alternative to design (rather than what sets up the alternative of design and chance) leads Dawkins to assert that the anthropic principle proves that chance explains the emergence of DNA on Earth in the already-mentioned statistical demonstration that life must have arisen on a billion planets.

In this regard, we should note that Dawkins is misapplying the anthropic principle in another sense. The anthropic principle normally refers to the fine-tuning of the original conditions at the universe's beginning; he is leaping ahead to the emergence of DNA much later. This actually hurts Dawkins' case further. If the initial conditions of the universe are finely-tuned, that fine-tuning makes possible any randomly-contrived chemical complexity that could occur only much later. If the correct inference from fine-tuning at the origin of the universe is divine design, then anything that occurs later, even by chance, occurs within the parameters of design.

We shouldn't be surprised, then, that when we do apply the notion of anthropic fine-tuning to DNA, the situation becomes even worse for Dawkins. If we fill in the gaps between the universe's original fine-tuning and the multiple layers of finely-calibrated conditions that must be met on every level (from galactic, to solar, and finally to planetary) to produce the conditions that would allow for DNA and life on a planet, we find the odds against life growing much larger than Dawkins' billion to one, and the number of possible planets meet-

9   Richard Dawkins, *The God Delusion*, 137.

ing these necessary, finely-calibrated conditions much smaller than Dawkins' billion billion.[10]

Dawkins misses all this precisely because he misapplies the anthropic principle in so many senses, beginning with his incorrect presentation of it as a kind of statistical proof that chance was the cause of fine-tuning. The final absurdity is his assertion that "the beauty of the anthropic principle is that it tells us, against all intuition, that a chemical model need only predict that life will arise on *one* planet in a billion billion to give us a good and entirely satisfying explanation for the presence of life here."[11]

Well, *that* makes it simple, doesn't it? You don't actually need concrete evidence; you only need a theoretical model that gives you good enough odds. You know it's correct because, well, you're here! Even laying that aside, what we've seen above about DNA and proteins, allows us to understand Dawkins' reasoning to be even more absurd. The odds against getting even the simplest strand of DNA are astronomically much higher than a billion to one. Even if it were not so, the enormous gap that exists in complexity and organization between DNA and even the simplest cell makes his implied equation of getting something like DNA and having life[12] to be problematic in the extreme.

If Dawkins cannot assume without proof that chance indeed was the cause of the universe's stunning fine-tuning, then we are back to a question of probability framed within the anthropic principle rightly understood. Given that the universe is known to be fine-tuned to an extraordinary degree right from the beginning of the Big Bang and running all the way down to the exacting conditions that allow for life on

---

10  On this, see especially Peter Ward and Donald Brownlee, *Rare Earth: Why Complex Life Is Uncommon in the Universe* (New York: Copernicus, 2000).
11  Richard Dawkins, *The God Delusion*, 138.
12  Richard Dawkins, *The God Delusion*, 138.

Earth, which is the more likely explanation of the miracle of life, an Intelligent God or Blind Chance?

Here, we must invoke our maxim: *No event that is more miraculous than the miracle that it seeks to discredit can be used as an explanation to deny that a miracle actually occurred.* Consider two possibilities: the fine-tuning of our universe by Blind Chance or an Intelligent Creator. If Blind Chance is a more improbable, more miraculous cause than God, then Dawkins' choice of Blind Chance as his anti-deity would violate this quite reasonable maxim. Unless blinded by devotion to God's non-existence, a reasonable person would infer that existence of a creative Intelligence as the cause of fine-tuning is far less miraculous than the aimless gropings of Chance.

There is evidence that Dawkins might, on some other level, realize this. He—like many others who have seen the handwriting on the cosmic wall—have latched onto a theory that seemingly allows us to escape the conclusion that the extraordinary fine-tuning of the universe implies a set-up job by a deity. Dawkins assumes that there are actually multiple universes, all of which have different parameters and laws. Of the billions upon billions of universes, only a very few—perhaps only one—has parameters and laws finely calibrated enough to allow for life. How do we know? Well, "of course, the present universe has to be one of that minority, because we are in it."[13]

Dawkins says of the "multiverse" theory that, even though he's read that "the idea is hated by most physicists....I think it is beautiful—perhaps because my consciousness has been raised by Darwin."[14] In other words, Dawkins believes the multiverse theory allows for natural selection among universes, thereby affirming the power of Darwinism in cosmology as well as biology. He doesn't mention the reason

---

13  Richard Dawkins, *The God Delusion*, 145.
14  Richard Dawkins, *The God Delusion*, 145.

most physicists would hate the multiverse theory: there is absolutely no evidence to support it, and in fact, no way ever to gather evidence for it since other hypothetical universes are obviously impossible to investigate or verify. In short, the multiverse theory is interesting in only one respect: it is good evidence of the desperation of both Dawkins and some physicists in wanting to avoid the obvious conclusion that fine-tuning of our universe demands a divine explanation. We have more evidence for fairies in our gardens, given that we at least have gardens.

If we might now move back again to the question of life's arising on Earth by the chance production of DNA, it is interesting to note Francis Crick's assessment of the possibility. Francis Crick, co-discoverer of the structure of DNA and every bit the atheist as Richard Dawkins, so despaired of the possibility of the chance production of the first cell that he put forth his famous panspermia thesis, that intelligent aliens must have seeded the Earth with life. Of course, he gave no explanation for their existence.

While not affirming Crick's aliens, we can see his logic: he understood that *some* kind of an intelligent cause was necessary because chance was powerless to achieve the results against such astronomical odds. Crick's despair forced him to this strange conclusion because the case against chance (and hence against Dawkins) is even stronger than we've let on. Crick's despair, then, is a sign that the chance production of life is *impossible* not improbable. Getting a cell by chance is not like getting dealt a perfect hand in bridge, but like throwing up a deck of cards in a hurricane and having it come down as a perfect card house.

Why? To go into a bit more detail than we did above, even the most basic, the most simple cell, is a dauntingly complex *integrated* whole. As an analogy, think about a car. A car is actually much *less* complex than the simplest cell. The simplest car—say, an old Volkswagen Beetle—has a significant number of well-defined, quite particular parts needed in order to make it run. Even if, for some very strange reason, by mere chance all the parts gathered together in the same small area, they still wouldn't make a functional automobile. They can't function unless they are precisely *integrated*; that is, until the parts, all of which have been quite precisely made to fit in both function and form with all the other parts, are brought together in one whole. While in some instances the parts of a cell do undergo a kind of self-integration, these aspects of self-assembly should not be overstated since much of the self-assembly takes place in the precise temporal, spatial, and chemical context provided for by the cell itself.

Someone might still reply, "Just give them a whole lot of time, and eventually we'll get the lucky combination. It doesn't have to happen all at once, but just in tiny steps." The "tiny steps" solution—a favorite of Dawkins—creates its own problems in turn. The complexity of the combination, the number of steps, and the time needed are all inextricably bound together when chance is posited as the ultimate cause. The more complex something is, the greater the number of steps are needed to build it, and so the more time it will take; the more time it takes, the more likely the complex but non-functional pieces will degrade under the variety of adverse chemical conditions of the environment before they could ever enter functional wholes.

There is a second reason why the chance rise of life is impossible and not merely extremely improbable. If the parts must come before the whole, why would the parts be there at all? Chance doesn't plan anything, but the parts of cell, as the parts of a car, are themselves complex entities built up of smaller, well-calibrated parts. In a car, each layer of complexity, from the smallest to the largest parts, is built for the whole. But on Dawkins' view, there can be no "built for" in the chance production of the parts leading up to the cell. He needs a random shuffle, not a stacked deck. But why would such elaborate parts exist over long periods of time? The answer is that they wouldn't. Not only is there no credible reason why smaller parts would combine to make larger parts that were *precisely* calibrated for function in living wholes that don't exist yet, but even granting that they could exist, they would most likely degrade in the variable hostile environmental conditions before the long, slow march of chance could jostle them into the right combination. This isn't difficult to understand. Just as a heap of car parts sitting out in all kinds of weather degrade over time, so also complex proteins and DNA would have a natural tendency to degrade over time. In fact, it is the very structure of the cell itself, and its delicately maintained internal environment, that shields the complex internal parts of the cell from the forces outside the cell that would degrade them. Some important pieces might survive the ravages of time, but not enough to make a functioning cell.

The actual history of life on Earth presents an even greater difficulty: too little time for chance to have been the cause. The problem, as we recall, is not only that the universe has a definite age, but that the first cells arose on Earth almost as soon as it became possible for them to exist. Dawkins, as we know, could cry "What luck!" but that would be "luck"—if it can be termed luck at all—in the *exact* sense as a statue of the Virgin Mary waving her arm.

There are many other problems with all attempts to explain the rise of life by mere chance.[15] We think that it is not just unlikely; it is simply an impossibility, and to treat it otherwise is like dreaming of a perfect card house floating into place in a hurricane.

But even if we grant that it is not impossible, but only extremely unlikely, Dawkins is not off the hook, as the vast scientific literature

---

15  See Benjamin Wiker and Jonathan Witt, *A Meaningful World*, chap. 8 which has both a more detailed account and a bibliography of sources in the footnotes.

generated in the last three decades concerning the origin of life attests.[16] In the *God Delusion*, Dawkins just skips over the enormous difficulties pointed out in this literature, and without warrant assigns the probability of life arising by chance to be such that it would happen on a billion out of a billion billion planets.

We've said enough about the conditions that pertain before there is any life to evolve. But what about Dawkins on his own turf? What about evolution once life's gotten started? Dawkins makes clear in *The God Delusion* (and elsewhere) that he believes that "Darwinian evolution proceeds merrily once life has originated."[17] No matter how biologically complex something happens to be, evolution can easily get there by small steps. So (as he emphasizes repeatedly) we are not asking whether, say, a fully formed eye can just pop into existence in a previously eye-less animal, but whether successive minute variations in DNA can ever so gradually transform a patch of light sensitive skin to the kind of extremely complex eye such as human beings have.

To put it into the memorable form of his book *Climbing Mount Improbable*, those who view the mountainous improbability of the evolution of an eye (or a wing, or a heart) as an insurmountable obstacle to believing in the theory of evolution, need to understand that evolution doesn't leap up Mount Improbable in a single bound, a feat which, if it occurred, would imply a Superman behind it all. Darwinism solves the problem "by breaking the improbability up into small, manageable parts, smearing out the luck needed, going round the back of Mount

16 For an overview see Iris Fry, *The Emergence of Life on Earth: A Historical and Scientific Overview* (New Brunswick, NJ: Rutgers University Press, 2000); Noam Lahav, *Biogenesis: Theories of Life's Origins* (Oxford: Oxford University Press, 1999); Robert Shapiro, *Origins: A Skeptic's Guide to the Creation of Life On Earth* (New York: Summit, 1986); Fazale Rana and Hugh Ross, *Origins of Life* (Colorado Springs: NavPress, 2004); Stephen C. Meyer, "DNA and the Origin of Life: Information, Specification, and Explanation," in John Campbell and Stephen Meyer, *Darwinism, Design, and Public Education* (East Lansing, MI: Michigan State University Press, 2003), 223–285.
17 Richard Dawkins, *The God Delusion*, 137.

Improbable and crawling up the gentle slopes, inch by million-year inch."[18] This means, of course, that we don't need God to explain evolution. In fact,

> Only God would essay the mad task of leaping up the precipice [of Mount Improbable] in a single bound. And if we postulate him as our cosmic designer we are left in exactly the same position as when we started. Any Designer capable of constructing the dazzling array of living things would have to be intelligent and complicated beyond all imagining. And complicated is just another word for improbable—and therefore demanding of explanation.[19]

This is an interesting and important admission for Dawkins, even while it contains a questionable assumption. He admits that if nature does take evolutionary leaps, then a supernatural source would have to be involved. Or, to put it the other way around, the only way that chance and cumulative selection can explain evolution is if, and only if, evolution proceeds by the smallest imaginable steps. Since God-less evolution must be blind, it can only crawl on its hands and knees precisely because it cannot proceed by intelligent choice.

This connection to intelligence allows Dawkins, so he thinks, to eliminate a "Designer." Since, for him, intelligence *only* comes through evolution, then (on Dawkins' grounds) we've got to explain how it is that God Himself evolved! We'll treat this particular argument against the "Designer" in the next chapter. Here, we'd like to focus on the evolution of intelligence in a more general way, for it allows us to view a fundamental difficulty for Dawkins' account of evolution.

---

18  Richard Dawkins, *Climbing Mount Improbable* (New York: W. W. Norton, 1996), 77.
19  Richard Dawkins, *Climbing Mount Improbable*, 77.

In the just-quoted paragraph, Dawkins maintains that something that is intelligent must therefore be complicated, and "complicated is just another word for improbable." That is a very strange and questionable assumption. The plot of Jane Austen's *Pride and Prejudice* is complicated. In what sense is it improbable? By this, we do not mean how probable is it that someone like Elizabeth Bennet from a lower rung of the aristocracy in England could have married someone like Mr. Darcy from the highest rung. We are focusing on the improbability of the book *itself* as a complex novel and as it was written by its author. Can we properly infer that, because it is complicated, it is therefore improbable?

The answer is that it isn't either probable or improbable; the complexities of the novel weren't a matter of chance, but the intelligent choice of the author. So, at least in this case, complicated is *not* just another word for improbable. In fact, it is another word for intelligently constructed.

Dawkins would object, stating something like this. Of course the book was intelligently constructed, but its complexity can be *treated* as a matter of probability (so that complicated *is* another word for improbable). The book is a string of letters. The probability of each letter occurring (taking into account spaces and discounting capital letters and punctuation) is 1 in 27. Thus, we *could* calculate the probability of generating *Pride and Prejudice* randomly by simply multiplying $\frac{1}{27}$ x $\frac{1}{27}$ x $\frac{1}{27}$ and so on, space by space, until we get to the end of the book. Of course, it would be a very huge number, to say the least. How large? To get some idea, let's look at just the famous opening sentence: "It is a truth universally acknowledged, that a single man in possession of a good fortune must be in want of a wife." The chances of generating this single sentence randomly are $27^{115}$ or a bit over $4 \times 10^{164}$ to one against.

Anyone who has read Dawkins' *Blind Watchmaker* recognizes that this is precisely how he treats Shakespeare to illustrate a point about evolution. Taking off on the old saw that if a million monkeys could bang away on a million typewriters for a million years they would generate all the works of Shakespeare, he attempts to show how a short sentence from Shakespeare can be generated randomly by a computer if we allow for cumulative selection.[20] His point is that if a computer (acting like the famed typing monkey) can happen upon a Shakespearean sentence by chance, then the old saw rings true. And this means, he infers by analogy, that evolution working merely by chance and cumulative selection can generate meaningful DNA "letter" sequences by randomly shuffling A, G, C, T.

As it turns out, by the way, when researchers actually got around to testing the merits of the saw on a cage full of crested macaques at Paignton Zoo in England in 2002, they found that the monkeys did very little typing (their output over several months being merely a few pages which consisted, for the most part, of hundreds of s's), meted out a fair dose of computer abuse (we'll spare the readers the scatological details), and for the most part, entirely ignored the keyboard. Real monkeys don't generate much of anything literarily, let alone something of the caliber of Shakespeare.

But returning to our original question, our objection is not whether Dawkins *could* calculate the probability of randomly generating *Pride and Prejudice* or a sentence from Shakespeare, but with the very notion of calculating the probability at all as illuminative. As he would obviously admit, that is *not* how Austen's masterpiece was made. *Pride and Prejudice* was made by Austen's intelligent authorial choices, not by random, letter-by-letter, cumulative generation. Yet, even acknowledging this, it is possible to give another kind of explanation, one that relies on chance not intelligence. There are, then, two kinds of explanations of *Pride and Prej-*

---

20 See Dawkins, *The Blind Watchmaker*, 45–50. For a more detailed criticism see Wiker and Witt, *A Meaningful World*, chap. 2.

*udice*, and we happen to know which one is correct. The same is true in regard to evolution, he would point out: in this case, we happen to know that the correct explanation is chance and not intelligence.

But here we can raise an interesting question. In both cases, there are two choices, two kinds of explanations, intelligence and chance. In regard to evolution, might Dawkins be attempting to give explanations for the occurrence of things by chance that may well have actually happened in a different way, by intelligence? This is an important question because it highlights a key distinction between a possible explanation and an actual demonstration. It seems to us, at least, that as long as Dawkins thinks he can give some kind of an explanation by chance, he seems satisfied in thinking that it *must* have happened that way. But that would be a fundamental error. You *can* give an explanation for some event or entity as merely the result of chance (say, Austen's novel or a Shakespearean sonnet), in the same way that you could give a Marxist or Freudian explanation for it. But the real question should always be, all ideology aside, *how did it actually happen?*

This is all the more interesting because, in an important way, Dawkins reduces intelligence itself to a matter of chance (as his statement above from *Climbing Mount Improbable* about God being improbable implies). Dawkins would argue something like this. Yes, Austen's intelligence is the proximate explanation for the complicated plot of *Pride and Prejudice*, but the brain is responsible for Jane Austen's intelligence, and the brain is the end result of an improbable string of beneficial evolutionary mutations. Therefore, in regard to her brain, which is the ultimate cause of her intelligence, we rightly say that "complicated is just another word for improbable." The explanation for this improbable thing, the human brain, is unguided, anti-theistic evolution slowly shuffling DNA, and no matter how great the leap to human intelligence might be, we know that if we just go round the back of Mount Improbable, we can crawl "up the gentle slopes, inch by million-year inch."

That may sound convincing until we actually think and test concretely about *what* that might mean. To repeat our point made above, one that is even more vivid if set in the context of Dawkins' Mount Improbable analogy, the higher you've got to go, the longer it will take to crawl upwards inch by million-year inch. Even if it's only a mile up Mount Improbable, then at a million years an inch, you get up the back in about 63,360,000,000 years—over four and a half times the age of the universe. That's a problem.

Thus, vague analogies about inching our way up the backs of imaginary mountains cannot take the place of very concrete explanations of the actual speed of evolution and the actual height of the mountain to be scaled. The problem is all the more difficult because we are not talking about one mountain with a brainless creature at the bottom and a brain sitting on the top, but the continuous climb upward, from one Mount Improbable to the next, mountain after mountain, from the simplest cells at about 3½ billion years ago, to the horrifyingly complex, multi-cellular biped with a massively complex brain well over three billion years later.

Here is the difficulty. The more complex an effect that the brain produces (such as *Pride and Prejudice*), the more complex the brain itself must be. The more complex the brain is, the greater the number of Mount Improbables evolution would have to have climbed to have produced it, and so the longer it must have taken. But we only have so much time before we bump into the 3.5 billion year barrier when the first cell appeared. The only way around the predicament of time, is to speed up evolution, so that, quite literally, evolution is happening by leaps and bounds. That is not a problem for some kind of a *theistic* account of evolution (as even Dawkins admits), but it is for Dawkins' atheistic account. Since chance is the anti-God, it can only crawl up the successive Mount Improbables inch-by-blind-inch. We are not presuming to offer a theistic, evolutionary solution in this short book, but we think it is reasonable to point out how serious this difficulty is for Dawkins' anti-theistic account of evolution. It makes it reasonable to suggest that the issue has not been settled between the two rival explanations, intelligence and chance, and that an explanation in terms of chance faces significant obstacles.

There are other difficulties. We might well ask, since in his account evolution is blind, why should evolution go *up* at all? Why didn't it stop at bacteria? The answer for Dawkins is, of course, that it goes "up" only in the sense that some mutation in DNA provides some very slight, even imperceptible advantage for a particular creature in its particular environment. Given even that slight edge, the carrier of the advantageously mutated gene is naturally selected—meaning that it has a better chance to survive and breed—and so it passes on this lucky gene to its progeny, thereby bequeathing all the previously acquired advantageous traits of that kind of creature and its new one as well. That's the inch-by-inch factor of "cumulative selection" that builds up biological complexity.

That's a perfectly reasonable account in many respects, but again, what makes it reasonable is the inch-by-inch nature of the advantages. If it is reasonable, it is reasonable precisely because each advantage is (in nearly every instance) directly correlated, inch-by-inch, to some indirect or direct use for that particular creature in that particular environment. (We say "in nearly every instance" because we can admit that it would be possible for organisms to carry "helpful" mutations as neutral for some time, but this would be the exception rather than the rule.) What keeps evolution from leaping uphill is not that a leap might not be helpful to the creature, but that the genetic changes necessary to make such a leap are too multifarious and complex for it ever to occur in a single step. As Dawkins then rightly insists, beneficial genetic change must be correlated very closely with advantages, inch-by-inch.

Let's use an example. Cheetahs chase gazelles. Gazelles are very fast. It would make sense that slightly faster cheetahs would catch more gazelles, and hence be more likely to survive and pass on to their offspring the genes that allowed them to be slightly faster (and note, we're not talking about a "faster" gene, but a complex suite of genes connected to multiple muscle structures). This is entirely possible, and indeed we know that it happens even without knowing all the genetic details. After all, that is how we breed racehorses. But if we found a small population of cheetahs who could run 600 mph rather than 60, we'd have to seek another explanation for this advantage that so far surpasses direct utility. What is going 600 mph *for*? It's just too big an evolutionary leap. If, in addition, these cheetahs regularly drew complex geometrical figures in the dirt with their sharp claws, and this in no way gave them any benefit for their survival, a strictly Darwinian-Dawkinsian explanation would fall flatter than flat.

The human brain presents us with both difficulties at once. It so far exceeds, in its powers, any direct use for mere survival, that there is no way to correlate an inch-by-inch crawl to particular concrete advantages for survival (and adding the notion that brainpower could be like the peacock's tail, an advantage in regard to sexual attractiveness, and hence natural sexual selection, is laughable). Moreover, human beings use their brains for entirely theoretical purposes that, however beautiful, are useless. A certain amount of brainpower would, of course, be an advantage, as the more clever animals illustrate. But we are not far different in our strangeness—we human animals—than the imaginary cheetahs merrily doing Euclidean geometry in the dirt. We regard such abstract knowledge as worthwhile in itself, even though it puts no supper on the table. As physicist Paul Davies notes, "We have certain skills—for example, we can jump streams and catch falling apples—which are necessary for getting by in the world, but why is it that we also have the ability to discern, for example, what's going on inside atoms or inside black holes? These are completely outside the domain of everyday experience...not at all necessary for good Darwinian survival."[21] To have a power that so exceeds the explanation of Darwinian natural selection is not a problem for some kind of *theistic* account of evolution, but the very thing that drives evolution up Mount Improbable for Dawkins can make no sense of such an enormous discrepancy between what is needed to survive, and the intellectual ability we've actually got. At least we can say this: because of the difficulties facing Dawkins' account, it is reasonable to hold that there are two alternative evolutionary explanations, intelligence and chance, and the case hasn't been decided in terms of chance.

So, we can see that the disagreement between theists and Dawkins, then, is not about the universe being 13.5 billion years old or that evolution of some kind has occurred. Both are entirely compatible with a theistic account of the universe, and hence present no difficulty for Catholics. The problem with Dawkins is his against-all-odds insistence that chance be the blind god who brings everything about.

It is this insistence that drives him into the several absurdities that we have noted, and the cause is always the same. His prejudice—prejudgment—against God. He seems intent on *any* explanation, as long as it doesn't allow for God. Again and again, that brings him to violate our most reasonable maxim, *No event that is more miraculous than the miracle that it seeks to discredit can be used as an explanation to deny that a miracle actually occurred.* Whether it concerns the origin of the universe, its fine-tuning, or the evolution of human intelligence, he would

---

21  Quoted in Benjamin Wiker and Jonathan Witt, *A Meaningful World*, 86.

rather his *credo* lead *ad absurdum,* than have it be a *credo in Deum, Patrem omnipotentem, Creatorem caeli et terrae.*[22] We wonder how much pride there is in his prejudice.

---

22 "I believe in God, the Father almighty, Creator of heaven and earth."

# 3

# Dawkins' Fallacious Philosophy

## Testing God and Doubting Thomas

We have covered the scientific aspects of Dawkins' attempt to show that belief in God is a delusion, and found that Dawkins' science is largely infected with an irrational faith in Chance as the anti-God. What about his attempts at philosophy? Philosopher Alvin Plantinga nicely quipped, in his review of *The God Delusion*, that some of Dawkins' "forays into philosophy are at best sophomoric, but that would be unfair to sophomores; the fact is (grade inflation aside), many of his arguments would receive a failing grade in a sophomore philosophy class."[1] Atheist philosopher Thomas Nagel also referred to Dawkins' attempts here as those of an "amateur," and his efforts "particularly weak."[2] We find ourselves concurring.

Dawkins' use of philosophy is, of course, to show the reader that time-honored proofs of God's existence fail, and that, for all practical and even impractical purposes, it can be demonstrated that God does not exist. Yet, he pulls up short of asserting that he can demonstrate absolutely that God does not exist. Why?

---

1  Alvin Plantinga, "The Dawkins Confusion: *Naturalism ad absurdum*," *Books and Culture* (http://www.christianitytoday.com/bc/2007/002/1.21.html).

2  Thomas Nagel, review of *The God Delusion*, "The Fear of Religion," *The New Republic* (10/23/2006): 25–29; quotes from p. 25.

"That you cannot prove God's non-existence is accepted and trivial," Dawkins informs his readers, "if only in the sense that we can never absolutely prove the non-existence of anything." To use an example Dawkins borrows from Bertrand Russell, we cannot disprove the existence of a microscopically small china teapot revolving around the sun between Earth and Mars because, in this hypothetical example, the existence of the thing in question is undetectable by any known means, and so the non-existence is impossible to prove. That shouldn't bother us, however. "None of us feels an obligation to disprove any of the millions of far-fetched things that a fertile or facetious imagination might dream up," such as the orbiting china teapot, or just as fantastically, an "invisible, intangible, inaudible unicorn," or the "Flying Spaghetti Monster." Yet, one "undisprovable" thing is worthy of the effort of our attention, God. "What matters is not whether God is disprovable (he isn't) but whether his existence is *probable*."[3]

Why does it matter? Why is it any more necessary to go after the undisprovable God, rather than after undetectable teapots or unicorns? One obvious answer would be that the number of people who believe in undetectable teapots or invisible, intangible, inaudible unicorns is negligible, but the number of people that believe in God is nearly uncountable. If you take the position that all or nearly all evil is religious at root, then you've got a good moral reason to hack and whittle away at the probabilities of God's existence. As Dawkins says, God is not just "a delusion," but "a pernicious delusion."[4] We'll attend to Dawkins' moral case against religion in later chapters. But here we want to note two other important reasons Dawkins cannot just leave the undisprovable God alone.

---

3   Richard Dawkins, *The God Delusion*, 51–54.
4   Richard Dawkins, *The God Delusion*, 31.

First, the undisprovable God really isn't like the undetectable teapot or unicorn. As Dawkins very clearly and very correctly points out, "a universe with a creative superintendent would be a very different kind of universe from one without."[5] For this reason, "The presence or absence of a creative super-intelligence is unequivocally a scientific question, even if it is not in practice—or not yet—a decided one."[6] Unlike an undetectable teapot or unicorn, the footprints of a Creator God should be somehow evident in creation if He exists, and likewise, if He doesn't exist, the absence of a Creator God should somehow be evident in the universe. Each would be a very different kind of universe. Given this quite reasonable assumption, Dawkins sets as his book's aim to disprove the proposition that "there exists a superhuman, supernatural intelligence who deliberately designed and created the universe and everything in it, including us."[7] That is an admirable aim, for one of the best ways to prove that the universe must have had a creative superintendent, is to throw all our efforts into trying to prove that it didn't. Let nature speak for itself.

What does nature seem to be saying? That brings us to the second reason Dawkins cannot leave the undisprovable God alone. On Dawkins' own admission, at least in his own discipline of biology, nature *seems* to be saying that "there exists a superhuman, supernatural intelligence who deliberately designed and created the universe and everything in it, including us." In his *Blind Watchmaker* he famously defines the science of biology as "the study of complicated things that give the appearance of having been designed for a purpose."[8] As he makes clear in example after example, there are many biological traits that give every appearance of having been designed by a super-human intelligence

---

5   Richard Dawkins, *The God Delusion*, 55.
6   Richard Dawkins, *The God Delusion*, 58–59.
7   Richard Dawkins, *The God Delusion*, 31. Italics in the original removed.
8   Richard Dawkins, *Blind Watchmaker*, 1.

(e.g., echolocation in bats), but once we dig more deeply, using our most up-to-date knowledge of how evolution works, we find that natural selection provides a perfectly sufficient explanation. We find out we don't need a Divine Designer after all. The blind watch-making powers of natural selection will do quite nicely.

Putting both reasons together, we now realize more clearly why Dawkins believes he must spend his time battling the undisprovable God, rather than attacking Flying Spaghetti Monsters, microscopic teapots, and undetectable unicorns. As he notes in his *God Delusion*, "We live on a planet where we are surrounded by perhaps ten million species, each one of which independently displays a powerful illusion of apparent design."[9] Since things in nature give the strong appearance of having been made by "a superhuman, supernatural intelligence who deliberately designed and created the universe and everything in it, including us," we are naturally inclined to believe in God.

We see, then, that Dawkins' rhetoric is charmingly misleading. Whatever his deeper intent, the rhetorical presentation of his argument leads the reader into thinking that the belief in God is equivalent to the belief in undetectable flying teapots: both are "undisprovable" and hence equally foolish. But then he goes on to assert that the universe would have to be a very different way if it were created by a supernatural intelligent being, whereas the existence or non-existence of a microscopic teapot (one could safely assume) would not have any effect on the universe one way or the other. On top of all this, we find that, in fact, living things have every appearance of being designed by a supernatural intelligent being. That puts Dawkins in an interesting position, quite the reverse of the one he implied. Since complicated biological things at least *appear* to be designed by an intelligent being, then it would be foolish (until one had better evidence) to believe that they were not.

---

9   Richard Dawkins, *The God Delusion*, 139.

So, once we strip away the rhetoric, all that Dawkins can really be saying is something like this: Until very recently in human history—up to the mid-19th century, i.e., the time before Darwin (B.D.)—any reasonable person would have concluded that there exists a superhuman, supernatural intelligence who deliberately designed and created the universe and everything in it, including us. Yet, some time after Darwin (A.D.), we began to uncover more and more evidence that such apparent design can be reduced to the blind workings of evolution, and so it became more and more reasonable to accept the existence of God as less and less probable.

Given that, let's examine the caliber of his philosophical arguments that would presumably drive home why Dawkins believes that it is more and more reasonable to accept the existence of God as less and less probable. Some of Dawkins' arguments are based on poor premises, one in particular on the poor premises shared by Dawkins and some well-intentioned believers in a "prayer experiment."[10] The reasoning goes something like this. If a personal God exists, then he always answers prayers. People pray for things. If they do get them, then God must exist; if they don't get them, then God must not exist. We should then be able to test whether or not God exists by doing a double-blind prayer experiment, where a percentage of a group of sick people are prayed for, but neither the sick nor the doctors know which ones are being prayed for, and even the people doing the praying only know the first name and last initial of the person for whom they are praying. As Dawkins notes with great satisfaction, an experiment of just such a kind failed to show any correlation between prayer and cure.

Dawkins rightly expresses contempt at this "whole barmy exercise," but apparently agrees with those who financed and undertook it

---

10  Richard Dawkins, *The God Delusion*, 61–66.

that such is exactly how one could test the alleged power of prayer. In short, he shares the same premises, even as an atheist.

There are two related errors in this type of reasoning, and the reasons for looking into them in some detail stretch far beyond the prayer experiment. First, it confuses a necessary causal link with a personal causal link. If the pressure and temperature of a gas are proportional, then when we increase pressure, temperature will increase as well. That is a necessary causal link. A personal causal link is quite different but no less real. The existence of a benefactor and getting a grant from a benefactor to write a book are causally linked, but we do not measure the existence or non-existence of benefactors by whether more or less than 50% of the monetary requests are granted. The difference is simple to understand. The gas is not free to permit or refuse the increase in temperature; the benefactor, for a nearly uncountable number of reasons unknown to the suppliant, may either affirm or deny his petition.

The error of the double-blind prayer experiment is that it treats God like some kind of natural cause, rather than as a personal, rational Being. In doing so, God is being unjustly subjected to a humiliating attempt to manipulate Him by an experiment. In short, the experiment is an insult, and any rational being, superhuman or not, would treat it as such. That does not, of course, mean that praying for healing itself is an insult; we are speaking only of framing such prayer in the context of a manipulative experiment.

But if there is a God, Dawkins would surely reply, then He is good, and a good God would always cure whoever asks Him for a cure in the same way that a doctor cures whoever comes to him.

This reveals a second error. The double-blind prayer experiment was not set up to test God, a superhuman, supernatural intelligence, with an entirely benevolent will, but only one aspect of God, His omnipotence. The test was to find out whether God will do what *we* think best; that is, it was a good test for the existence of a genie, but not for the existence of God.

This requires some elaboration. Genies are like powerful machines, such as computers or sophisticated bombs. These machines do *exactly* as we bid them, for better or worse, good or evil, because they are not *persons* with wisdom and a benevolent will matching their respective powers. They are powerful *things* with no wisdom to discern what is actually good and no desire to put it into effect. The machine does exactly what *we* think best. A genie does much the same thing. He does not consider the caliber of the request; it may even cause the misery and destruction of the one doing the requesting. He merely says, "Your wish is my command," which is, for better or worse, to yoke the genie's omnipotence to the petitioner's intelligence and will.

We can now see a bit better why we can't "test" for God this way. To test for something, if a test is indeed possible, we have to test for what the thing *really is*. If a superhuman, supernatural intelligent personal Being exists, we cannot just test for omnipotence because omnipotence isn't the Being. In God, supernatural power would be essentially united to supernatural intelligence and a supernatural, benevolent will. (Strictly speaking, from the theological point of view, in God these things cannot even be isolated; as theologians maintain, in God wisdom, power, and love are identical. That is the most profound reason that we cannot merely "test" for one.)

We don't need to be God, however, to understand this. Any good parent can. As fathers or mothers, we don't grant every request made by our children, even though we have the *power* to do what they ask; in fact, we deny quite a few requests because we *know* that answering them would not be good for the child and, since we *love* the child, we don't want any harm to come to him or her. Furthermore, good parents consider "harm" in many senses other than merely physical harm (as Dawkins himself does, given his chapter against "brainwashing" children by religious indoctrination).

Having said all that, it is clear that Dawkins and nearly everyone else would still be unsatisfied. "Whatever the merits of your point," he might say, "no father would refuse to cure his cancer-ridden child if the child asked him and if he indeed had the power to do so; no mother would refuse to save her drowning child, even without being asked, if indeed she had the power to do so."

That is a most serious objection, one that is faced all the more poignantly by believers rather than non-believers. We will return to this important objection. But here, our philosophical focus is on God's existence, not on His benevolence. First things first. God cannot be benevolent if He does not exist. However, we can at least imagine that a superhuman, supernatural intelligence could exist who was entirely indifferent to human affairs. And so, our analysis of prayer and its efficacy leads us to a more basic question (one that will ultimately help us better answer the poignant objection).

Our first step will be a rather strange one, to say the least. We should like the reader to take with the utmost seriousness a question that formed the basis for a now-famous article by philosopher Thomas Nagel, "What is it like to be a bat?"[11] Nagel's article is a classic, and Dawkins himself refers to it in his discussion of echolocation in bats in *Blind Watchmaker*.[12]

What is the point of asking such an odd question? Nagel's point is both simple and far more profound than it first appears. Human beings discern the presence and character of objects with their eyes using waves of light. Bats do the same thing, except that they do it through

---

11 Thomas Nagel, "What is it like to be a bat?" *The Philosophical Review* LXXXIII, 4 (October 1974), 435–450. Happily, this article is online at several locations.
12 Richard Dawkins, *Blind Watchmaker*, 33.

sound waves using echolocation. But when we say "the same thing," we mean only that vision and echolocation "serve the same function," not that a bat's experience of three-dimensional reality is the *same as* our experience of three-dimensional reality. The truth is, we are forever cut off from knowing what it is like to be a bat because "bat sonar, though clearly a form of perception, is not similar in its operation to any sense that we possess, and there is no reason to suppose that it is subjectively like anything we can experience or imagine." Nagel continues,

It will not help to try to imagine that one has webbing on one's arms, which enables one to fly around at dusk and dawn catching insects in one's mouth; that one has very poor vision, and perceives the surrounding world by a system of reflected high-frequency sound signals; and that one spends the day hanging upside down by one's feet in an attic. In so far as I can imagine this (which is not very far), it tells me only what it would be like for *me* to behave as a bat behaves. But that is not the question. I want to know what it is like for a *bat* to be a bat. Yet if I try to imagine this, I am restricted to the resources of my own mind, and those resources are inadequate to the task. I cannot perform it either by imagining additions to my present experience, or by imagining segments gradually subtracted from it, or by imagining some combinations of additions, subtractions, and modifications.[13]

We must make every effort not to confuse, warns Nagel, "having the same function" and "having the same experience," a confusion in which Dawkins seems carelessly to indulge in his *Blind Watchmaker* by his "conjecture" that human vision and bat echolocation are "translated" by an "inner computer" into "the same kind of nerve impulses on its way

---

13  Thomas Nagel, "What is it like to be a bat?"

to the brain" so that "bats 'see' in much the same way as we do."[14] Obviously Dawkins either misses or dismisses Nagel's point: since we can't experience things by echolocation, we can't *know* that the bat is having the same subjective experience of the outside world; in fact, since the way it perceives is so different, we have every reason to believe that its subjective experience is wholly alien to ours. Furthermore, in Dawkins' conjecturing that bats "see" in much the same way we do, he is merely imagining what it would be like for Richard Dawkins "to behave [or perceive] as a bat behaves [or perceives]." "But that is not the question," Nagel reminds the reader. "I want to know what it is like for a *bat* to be a bat," not Richard Dawkins to be a bat.

What has all this to do with God? Let's change Nagel's question to this. "What is it like to be God?" This question cannot be answered by imagining God as an infinitely magnified human being any more than we can know what it would be like to be a bat by imagining ourselves with webbed arms, poor vision, perceiving things by sonar, flitting about at night catching insects, and hanging upside down in an attic during the day.

We come up against the same insuperable obstacle in both instances. In regard to a bat, since we can have no access to the inner experience of a being with such a radically different mode of perception, we are really doing little more than dressing ourselves up in a bat suit. Similarly, we cannot know what it is like to perceive and act as God perceives and acts by imagining *ourselves* with the power to do anything. That is merely to imagine an infinitely magnified version of ourselves. But the simple truth is that we are not omniscient, omnipotent, omnibenevolent, purely spiritual beings any more than we are bats.

We may now see why we took this particular "tangent" from the discussion of the double-blind prayer experiment. Again, there is an ob-

14  Richard Dawkins, *Blind Watchmaker*, 34–35.

vious relationship between what we "test" for, and what we think the thing *is* that we are "testing" for. This holds true for Dawkins' attempt to "test" for God in his book. We have good reason to suspect that Richard Dawkins is testing the universe for the existence of an infinitely magnified Richard Dawkins. Small wonder that he didn't find one.

Lest the reader think we are merely being glib, one of Dawkins' favorite "proofs" for the non-existence of God, which he repeats several times triumphantly throughout *The God Delusion*,[15] is that no philosophical or scientific proof of an intelligent first cause is possible because it must always collapse into an infinite regress. (Such was the gist of his gibe that we quoted from *Mount Improbable* in the last chapter: "Any Designer capable of constructing the dazzling array of living things would have to be intelligent and complicated beyond all imagining. And complicated is just another word for improbable—and therefore demanding of explanation.")

Let's now examine this claim in more detail. As he repeats in *The God Delusion*, things that are complex enough to be intelligent, must themselves be the products of evolution.[16] Therefore, maintains Dawkins, if a superhuman intelligence exists, then it too must have been the product of an evolutionary process, and if we posit that some other superhuman intelligence must have somehow been the cause of that evolutionary process, well then that intelligence must also have been the product of an evolutionary process, and so on *ad infinitum, ad absurdum*. And so, for Dawkins, the notion of God presents us with an inescapable problem, infinite regress. So, even if we can't disprove Him, we must at least admit that His existence is "very very improbable indeed."[17]

---

15  Richard Dawkins, *The God Delusion*, 109, 114, 120, 141, 143, 147, 155–156.
16  Richard Dawkins, *The God Delusion*, 31, 73.
17  Richard Dawkins, *The God Delusion*, 109.

On the contrary. This argument, which Dawkins takes to be a real zinger, is entirely fallacious, and the problem is a variation of the one noted above: just as imagining oneself doing what a bat does, will not allow one to know what it is like to be a bat, so also imagining God's intelligence as a really, really powerful version of our intelligence, does not allow us to know what it is like to be a purely spiritual, omniscient Being. Thinking that it does brings Dawkins to assume that all intelligence must exist exactly like his mode of intelligence (granting for the moment that he is correct in the way that he characterizes even his own intelligence).

How does this relate to God's "improbability"? Dawkins clearly imagines God to be a creature like him whose intelligence he believes to be purely material in function and purely evolutionary in origin. Since he believes that his own intellectual capacities are the result of material evolutionary processes, therefore *all* possible intelligent beings, including God, *must* be the result of material evolutionary processes. Because evolution, for Dawkins, is always a matter of chance material mutation, then he can treat the existence of intelligence as a matter of probability and improbability, even the existence of an intelligent God. This is the same mode of error we pointed out in the last chapter, using *Pride and Prejudice* to illustrate.

What, then, does Dawkins actually prove? Again, at best he has shown that an infinitely magnified Richard Dawkins cannot have been the cause of the universe. Of that, we are already well aware. Thomas Nagel (who is himself an atheist) faults Dawkins on this very confusion in his review of *The God Delusion*.

But God, whatever he may be, is not a complex physical inhabitant of the natural world [as Dawkins defines Him]. The explanation of his existence as a chance concatenation of atoms [via evolution] is not a possibility for which we must find an alternative, because that is not what anybody means by God. If the God hypothesis [as put forth by theists] makes sense at all, it offers a different kind of explanation from those of physical science: purpose or intention of a mind without a body, capable nevertheless of creating and forming the entire physical world. The point of the hypothesis is to claim that not all explanation is physical, and that there is a mental, purposive, or intentional explanation more fundamental than the basic laws of physics, because it explains even them[18]

---

We agree with Nagel. Dawkins' proof would only work if we were in search of "a supremely adept and intelligent natural being, with a super-body and a super-brain,"[19] but again, that is not what anybody means by God. Consequently, "What is it like to be God," is not answered by saying, "Pretty much like what it is to be Richard Dawkins, only more so." The Being that we are attempting to prove or disprove is a very different kind of intelligent being. Dawkins' "zinger" proof is about as effective as someone trying to prove that echolocation doesn't exist in bats because the only way to discern objects that *we* experience is vision.

We now see the importance of our pointing out earlier that God is a necessary Being by definition. He is necessary, in part, because He is outside of physical contingency, outside the realm of chance. It is only in Dawkins' treating God as having an evolved, material intelligence that allowed him the dubious luxury of discounting His existence as very, very improbable. As Nagel rightly drives home, since God is by definition purely spiritual, then the contingency of material atom-shuffling is inapplicable, and therefore, the very idea of treating God as improbable is entirely misconstrued.

---

18  Thomas Nagel, "The Fear of Religion," 26.
19  Thomas Nagel, "The Fear of Religion," 26.

Again, we cannot move, without argument, from God being *defined* as having necessary existence to God necessarily existing, but the horns of Dawkins' dilemma in this regard are as fictional as a unicorn's. There simply is no problem with infinite regress in the way that Dawkins maintains. At best, Dawkins would be providing a good proof against anyone (like Francis Crick) who posited intelligent aliens as the designers of our world.

We may now return to the prayer experiment, with perhaps a little more insight into its misconceptions. In order to "frame" the test correctly, we would want to ask what would appear to be an impossible question to answer, and our inability to answer it would seem to undermine the whole enterprise. "What is it like to be a purely spiritual being, all-knowing, all-powerful, all-loving, who understands immediately and completely all the ramifications of any action throughout all time and for eternity, and takes into account in any decision, all these ramifications, including the physical *and* spiritual good that would result, not just in regard to any single person praying, but in regard to everyone and everything in the present and the indefinite future who would be affected?" That is the God to be "tested," not an evolved genie. And here is the great difficulty that follows from it. Given the scope of God's defined knowledge, power, and benevolence, *any* result could be perfectly compatible with such a God having answered all the prayers in terms of what was truly good for each petitioner as calibrated along with the good of all present and future human beings.

This may be difficult to understand until we take the larger scope of things, that is, the larger context of multiple, intersecting, interrelated goods of every level, and not just the immediate physical good involved in healing. Even a doctor, who must heal all those who ask him, often sees conflicts between the patient's larger good and the good of those around him, and mere physical healing. A patient dying of emphysema wants to be cured (a physical good), but he doesn't want to give up smoking. An alcoholic wants her liver to be cured, but she doesn't want to give up drinking. A man wants to be patched up after an automobile accident, but he won't give up driving recklessly and endangering the lives of others. A woman with cancer has made everyone around her miserable for decades, and will continue to do so for many more if cured. A man with cancer, who has likewise made everyone around him miserable for decades, finally realizes, in the face of impending death, how much wrong he has done and how much good he could have done. A doctor sees these complexities every day. How much more could an omniscient God see?

That is all the more important a question when we take into account the spiritual good of the patient. Since, as we've argued, we are testing for a purely spiritual God, then it is also permissible to take into account in the test, the spiritual good of the patient. Dawkins, as a materialist, can only test for a material cure and a material good, but a theist takes into account both a spiritual and material good, and does so with a definite ranking: spiritual above material. This means, of course, that for the Christian, the ultimate cure of every physical malady is indeed death, and the ultimate good against which any material good (including the cure of a disease) is measured is eternal life. For Christians, this is brought to a profound point in the crucifixion of Jesus Christ, which lifts up before them the startling and difficult doctrinal truth that physical suffering and death were the means for achieving the ultimate spiritual good (a means that the believer, too, is called in embrace in imitation of Christ). This is, of course, difficult enough for the Christian to accept and, since Dawkins as a materialist must measure all goods as physical, it is impossible for him to accept. But that is the God being tested. The answer to the most poignant objections about physical suffering and death, and God not answering prayers, cannot satisfy Dawkins, for the answer is Christ Himself, the Christ who sweated blood, who asked if it be possible that the cup should pass from Him, Who cried out on the cross about being forsaken. This is also the Christ of the resurrection. There are no easy, end-arounds for the Christian, and the worst case of prayers not being answered drive the believer to assume an often unwilling imitation of Christ. But the larger context of understanding is provided by the resurrection, the context in which all questions about the ultimate good must be placed.

Given this much larger spiritual, eternal context, we can see again why it is difficult to assess whether God had indeed answered the prayers of petitioners in light of their true good, present and future, as inextricably bound up with the good of an indefinite number of others. That is not to say that the experiment therefore proves God's existence *whatever* the result, or on the contrary, that since any result is possible, then no result would prove that there was a God who answers prayers. Obviously, if everyone who was actually prayed for *was* then instantaneously healed (contrary to Dawkins' waving Virgin Mary statue logic), we would accord it all to be miraculous. Although Dawkins states that such would be a proof of the existence of a God who answers prayers, one wonders if he would simply regard it as good luck. That is, of course, another reason the experiment wouldn't "work." Dawkins' inflated faith in chance would lead him, so it would seem, to reject all obvious miracles as non-miraculous. If indeed Dawkins would change his mind upon witnessing a miracle, then he would have to accept the larger context into which the miracle-producing Christian God fits (and that would mean, one would think, rejecting the prayer experiment as misconceived).

However that may be, even Dawkins would have to admit, for entirely different reasons, a larger context of good against which individual requests must be measured. On his own terms, that is, in the context of evolution, death is a way of weeding out the unfit, and the destruction of individuals is fully in accord with the larger evolutionary and environmental whole. In regard to the larger environmental good, the interconnectedness of a delicately balanced ecosystem means that what may appear to be good for particular individuals, may actually throw the entire system into ecological imbalance, bringing destruction for both the individuals who caused the imbalance and for a good many other, entirely innocent creatures. Human beings are particular adept at causing environmental harm, given that their selfishness and short-sightedness are magnified geometrically by the powers of technology. If Dawkins found himself on the other side of the prayer experiment, in charge of affirming or denying petitions, he would have to take all this into account, and this includes decisions about life and death, since in general people want to go on living when it might be better, from a purely material medical and evolutionary view, that they die. No doubt Dawkins would make quite different decisions about life and death than the Christian God but he would find himself having to make the same kind of decisions.

Let us leave the prayer experiment behind, and move on. What about Dawkins' other philosophical disproofs of God's existence? Dawkins lavishes several pages of ridicule on St. Anselm's argument for God's existence,[20] without realizing that it was St. Thomas himself (whom Dawkins skewers first) who had long ago rejected Anselm's proof for much the same reasons as Dawkins.[21] To his philosophical credit, Dawkins sees the same kinds of problems that St. Thomas did.

Yet, there the affinity with St. Thomas ends. Dawkins' refutations of St. Thomas Aquinas' famous five proofs of God's existence are painfully breezy. He dismisses three of them because "they make the

---

20  To be all too short, we conceive of God as all-perfect; but it is more perfect to exist than not exist; therefore, the proper conception of God necessarily includes existence; therefore God exists.
21  Thomas Aquinas, *Summa Theologiae*, I.2.1, ad 2.

---

entirely unwarranted assumption that God himself is immune to regress."[22] This criticism misses the point of the proofs.

Each of St. Thomas' three proofs makes the exact same kind of assumption that was made by scientists in the 20th century who inferred from the present state of the universe's expansion, that if one "played" the expansion backwards, one would come to a "singularity," a "point" which has to be considered an origin but which is outside space, time, and the domain of the laws of nature, and which itself must either be a cause or have a cause because the universe cannot come from nothing. Contrary to Dawkins' claim, the focus in St. Thomas' proofs is actually on the way that nature presents itself to us, not on the notion of infinite regress itself. "Since we see that everything in nature is contingent (St. Thomas' third proof), then something non-contingent will ultimately have to ground the contingent," is the same kind of reasoning as, "Since the universe is expanding, then it must have arisen from an infinitely dense 'point.'"

If St. Thomas is wrong in using this kind of proof, then Dawkins must likewise reject the kind of reasoning that led to the revelation of the Big Bang. In each case, because of the way nature itself is, we find that we must have a "terminator" (to use Dawkins' inapt word), something that is other than nature as we know it, and that exists as a cause of nature as we know it. Furthermore, St. Thomas adds, in each of the proofs, something like, "This all men speak of as God," and *not* "This *is* God." The reason for this is important: there is a significant difference between knowing *that* there must be such a cause, and identifying *who* or *what* that cause is. Some philosophical distance must therefore be kept between the bare recognition through a very particular proof that there must be an ultimate cause outside of nature, and the nature of the cause itself.

---

22 Richard Dawkins, *The God Delusion*, 77.

Dawkins loads confusion on confusion by not understanding this important point. "Even if we allow the dubious luxury of arbitrarily conjuring up a terminator to an infinite regress and giving it a name, simply because we need one," Dawkins avers, "there is absolutely no reason to endow that terminator with any of the properties normally ascribed to God: omnipotence, omniscience, goodness, creativity of design, to say nothing of such human attributes as listening to prayers, forgiving sins and reading innermost thoughts."[23] If Dawkins had taken the time to read St. Thomas carefully, he would have realized that (1) St. Thomas would agree that the bare demonstration does not permit one to infer all these attributes, and so they don't appear in the proofs, and that (2) some of these qualities can be reasonably inferred through further philosophical argument (e.g., God's omnipotence), while others could only be known through revelation (e.g., that God forgives sins).

We have spent some time on Dawkins' treatment of these proofs to illustrate a broader point. His treatment of St. Thomas is entirely too quick, and one suspects that the ease of his dismissal has to do with his contempt for his opponents. Since his adversaries have nothing to say, then they can be brushed off with a self-confident smirk. Terry Eagleton's review of *The God Delusion* captures the frustration of someone reading the book who actually knows the subject matter Dawkins rides over roughshod.

Imagine someone holding forth on biology whose only knowledge of the subject is the *Book of British Birds*, and you have a rough idea of what it feels like to read Richard Dawkins on theology. Card-carrying rationalists like Dawkins, who is the nearest thing to a professional atheist we have had since Bertrand Russell, are in one sense the least well-equipped to understand what

23 Richard Dawkins, *The God Delusion*, 77.

they castigate, since they don't believe there is anything there to be understood, or at least anything worth understanding. That is why they invariably come up with vulgar caricatures of religious faith that would make a first-year theology student wince. The more they detest religion, the more ill-informed their criticisms of it tend to be. If they were asked to pass judgment on phenomenology or the geopolitics of South Asia, they would no doubt bone up on the question as assiduously as they could. When it comes to theology, however, any shoddy old travesty will pass muster.[24]

But there is more wincing than that done by first year theology students, as the above should have made evident; the first year philosophy students would be giving an embarrassed shudder as well.

Not all Dawkins' attempts to deal with philosophical arguments are likewise unsatisfactory. Sometimes the confusion resides in his opponents, as in his treatment of "The Argument from Scripture."[25] As we made clear right from the start, since the Bible is a revealed text and the belief *that* it is revealed is a matter of faith, then (following St. Thomas' sage advice) it does no good to argue with a non-believers using Scripture as authoritative because they assume, as non-believers, that the text is not authoritative. To point out, for example, the fact that Isaiah prophesied accurately about Christ's life has no merit with someone who thinks the whole book, Old and New Testament alike, is a fairy tale. There is no point in wasting time with a non-believer, then, about more technical points concerning alleged contradictions in the Bible, or the findings of modern scriptural scholarship that would certainly seem to undermine the credibility of the sacred text. He would not believe that the text was revealed even if it were entirely free from the remot-

24 Terry Eagleton, "Lunging, Flailing, Mispunching," *London Review of Books* (October 19, 2006).
25 Richard Dawkins, *The God Delusion*, 92–97.

est hint of contradiction, or even if scriptural scholars unanimously affirmed the unity and veracity of the text.

Another instance of confusion in Dawkins' opponents is worth more of a look. In his consideration of "The Argument from Beauty"[26] he rightly rejects the riposte meant to silence the atheist, "How do you account for Shakespeare, then?" Or Mozart, Bach, Michelangelo, etc.? As Dawkins rightly replies, the bare argument from the existence of human-made beauty to God must be recognized as faulty, unless we want to affirm the existence of a bevy of contrarian Greek deities from the existence of the Parthenon. "If there is a logical argument linking the existence of great art to the existence of God, it is not spelled out by its proponents," complains Dawkins.[27]

That is not true. It is, for example, spelled out in significant detail in *A Meaningful World: How the Arts and Sciences Reveal the Genius of Nature* (Benjamin Wiker and Jonathan Witt). The subtlety of the argument does not make it amenable to a short presentation in this book, let alone a cavalier treatment such as Dawkins would likely give it. But one aspect of the argument is worth considering, even if in a summary way, the relationship of intellectual beauty *in science* to the existence of God. We offer it in the next chapter, but for now, let's finish out on Dawkins' arguments.

Dawkins fields three more kinds of philosophical arguments, "The Argument from Personal Experience," "The Argument from Admired Religious Scientists," and "Pascal's Wager."[28] In regard to the argument from personal experience, Dawkins rightly rejects it. We agree that a religious person's personal account of some mystical experience is not an argument for the existence of God, for the

---

26  Richard Dawkins, *The God Delusion*, 86–87.

27  Richard Dawkins, *The God Delusion*, 87.

28  Richard Dawkins, *The God Delusion*, 87–92, 97–103, 103–105. We leave out the "Bayesian Arguments," since we agree with Dawkins that it is an argument not worth either attacking or defending.

same reason that Dawkins' self-reported "quasi-mystical response to nature and the universe" that he characterizes as a form of "transcendent wonder"[29] is not an argument demonstrating that God does not exist. The reason is simple: a personal experience is not an argument for precisely the reason that it is personal.

"The Argument from Admired Religious Scientists" (e.g., Einstein believed that some kind of God existed, therefore…) is rightly rejected. But we would like to add that it must be cast aside for the same reason that we should reject Dawkins' attempt to slip in "The Argument from Admired Irreligious Scientists," wherein he glibly reports that most scientists are unbelievers. They are both to be rejected for the same reason that we should rebuff someone trying to prove a political position by "The Argument from Admired Tory Scientists" or "The Argument from Admired Democratic Scientists." As Dawkins himself has illustrated, there is no intrinsic connection between a scientist knowing a lot about a particular branch of science (say, biology) and his knowing a lot about theology, philosophy, politics, gardening, the history of China, or any other field that has a determinate body of knowledge that needs to be well understood before one can make a comment upon it. Just being a scientist is not enough. As Terry Eagleton has driven home, one must be familiar with the theological arguments, whatever one's capacities are as a scientist. Insofar as science itself can contribute to the question, we have already noted that Dawkins' scientific case against theism is weak precisely because his faith in chance is so strong. He greatly minimizes the difficulties raised by scientists surrounding origin of life research and misuses the anthropic principle to favor chance even though many scientists have seen it as providing new evidence in favor of theism.

And finally, we have Dawkins' treatment of "Pascal's Wager." The wager goes something like this. Even if we don't know that God exists,

---

29 Richard Dawkins, *The God Delusion*, 11–12.

it is safer to bet on it. If you are wrong, well, you've lived a good life anyway; and if you're right, you zip into heaven. It's a win-win, no-brainer. Of course, this short account does not do justice to the wager, which should be read in the context of Blaise Pascal's entire *Pensées*, but our point in relation to Dawkins can be made even with a caricature of Pascal. Dawkins takes the wager to be absurd for the very good reason that you can't just "believe" something merely because it seems like a useful policy. The most one could do in following Pascal's advice is to pretend to have belief.[30] Dawkins is right, and Christians should agree. Christian doctrine holds that faith, the capacity to believe what is above reason, is a gift of grace; feigning belief as a good bet is not the same as having real faith. Here, at least, Dawkins is entirely on the side of orthodoxy.

---

30  Richard Dawkins, *The God Delusion*, 104.

# 4

# Can God's Existence Be Demonstrated?

Science itself points to God.

So far we have concentrated on the negative task of showing how Dawkins' attempts to disprove the existence of God and prove the existence of a God-less universe are, upon inspection, faulty. We have not offered a proof of God's existence ourselves. Is there such a proof? Is there such a proof to which even Dawkins *himself* would have to assent?

The answer is yes and no. In that order. Yes, there is a proof, and no, it would not be likely to convince Dawkins himself, and the reason is that Mr. Dawkins is not rational enough. He follows reason up to a point, but it is a far too narrow point, one defined by his reductionism. Reductionism is a constriction of both reason *and* reality, one that paradoxically keeps the reductionist from giving an accurate account even of himself and closes off the possibility of understanding a demonstration of God's existence.

We can capture this paradox in a maxim that is worth keeping in mind when we talk about demonstrations of God's existence: *Any demonstration of God's existence or non-existence must be of such a kind as to allow both for the existence of the demonstrator and for the possibility of demonstration.*

For example, suppose a reductionist claims that miracles cannot occur because the universe is governed by the iron laws of nature. Since nature is entirely self-contained and determined, and the laws of nature are unbreakable, then miracles are impossible. Indeed, since nature is entirely self-contained and determined, there is no need of God. Therefore, the reductionist announces, not only are miracles impossible but God does not exist (or if He does, He is of no consequence, since His existence doesn't concern or affect us).

We lay aside the more subtle but real difficulties with the assumptions of this common reductionist position (such as the notion that there are things, "laws," that cause other things to happen, a point to which we'll return below), and take it as it is commonly set forth. On its own terms, this quite common "proof" violates the maxim, and so it proves nothing at all. If the reductionist were right, then he could not possibly know that he is right. He himself would be entirely determined by material causes both in his offering of this particular proof and in the various elaborate mechanical and energetic exchanges going on in his brain that make him *think* that his proof is convincing. He actually may be right, but of course, he cannot know. "Truth" and "being convinced" are not measures of reality; they are only *his* particular brain states as determined by the laws of nature. Demonstration therefore becomes impossible because every demonstration itself only plays out what the demonstrator has been determined to believe by the laws of physics.

This common "proof" violates the maxim on another level. Regardless of what he might say, no human demonstrator *lives* as an entirely determined being. He makes decisions about what to eat or not eat, what to say or not say, about how to word the demonstration, about when to go to bed, about what book he has on his nightstand and when to pick it up and read it, and so on. But in order to make miracles impossible, the reductionist has to contrive an entirely fanciful universe in which his own ordinary choices cannot take place. In that fanciful universe, deciding to have marmalade rather than apple butter on his morning toast is as miraculous as Jesus Christ raising Lazarus from the dead. Something is obviously awry with such a "proof."

We are not at all assuming Dawkins to follow the exact contours of this common but crude reductionist approach, but there is one aspect of such reductionism that does concern us in regard to Dawkins, one that violates this maxim in somewhat the same way.

As we recall, Dawkins denied that God could exist as an Intelligent Creator because any being with sufficient intelligence to create would Himself have to be a product of evolution, and hence would require an evolutionary explanation of the development of His intelligence in turn. In maintaining this, Dawkins was assuming that his reductionist, anti-theistic account of the evolution of human intelligence explained the level of intelligence that it takes for *him*—for Richard Dawkins—to offer his own demonstration of God's non-existence. But if it turns out that his reductionist, purely materialistic account of the evolution of intelligence can't tell us how Dawkins himself has the intelligence to demonstrate, then it is useless as part of a demonstration involving an evolutionary description of what Divine Intelligence would have to be.

We can begin to see this point about reductionism and intellectual demonstration more clearly on a far grander scale, and from a slightly different angle. In Stephen Hawking's celebrated *A Brief History of Time*, he states the following paradox that entangles anyone looking for a grand unified theory of everything in physics.

> Now, if you believe that the universe is not arbitrary, but is governed by definite laws, you ultimately have to combine the partial theories into a complete unified theory that will describe everything in the universe.

But there is a fundamental paradox in the search for such a complete unified theory. The ideas about scientific theories outlined above [in his book] assume we are rational beings who are free to observe the universe as we want and to draw logical deductions from what we see. In such a scheme it is reasonable to suppose that we might progress ever closer toward the laws that govern the universe. Yet if there really is a complete unified theory, it would also presumably determine our actions. And so the theory itself would determine the outcome of our search for it! And why should it determine that we come to the right conclusions from the evidence? Might it not equally well determine that we draw the wrong conclusions? Or no conclusion at all?[1]

Hawking admirably illustrates what we might offer as a corollary to the above maxim: *Any theory in science that includes the existence of the scientist must allow both for the existence of the scientist and science itself.* If science is about truth, then there must be something wrong with a theory that undermines the possibility that we can know whether a theory is true.

Hawking tries to wriggle his way out of the dilemma in a quite ridiculous way, one that brings us right back to Dawkins.

The only answer that I can give to this problem is based on Darwin's principle of natural selection. The idea is that in any population of self-reproducing organisms, there will be variations in the genetic material and upbringing that different individuals have. These differences will mean that some individuals are better able than others to draw the right conclusions about the world around them and act accordingly. These individuals will be more likely to survive and reproduce

---

1   Stephen Hawking, *A Brief History of Time* (New York: Bantam, 1988), 12.

and so their pattern of behavior and thought will come to dominate. It has certainly been true in the past that what we call intelligence and scientific discovery has conveyed a survival advantage. It is not so clear that this is still the case: our scientific discoveries may well destroy us all, and even if they don't, a complete unified theory may not make much difference to our chances of survival. However, provided the universe has evolved in a regular way, we might expect that the reasoning abilities that natural selection has given us would be valid also in our search for a complete unified theory, and so would not lead us to the wrong conclusions.[2]

Of course, this is nonsense on several counts. To repeat physicist Paul Davies insight about the limits of Darwinian explanation in regard to intelligence, "We have certain skills—for example, we can jump streams and catch falling apples—which are necessary for getting by in the world, but why is it that we also have the ability to discern, for example, what's going on inside atoms or inside black holes? These are completely outside the domain of everyday experience...not at all necessary for good Darwinian survival." We take it that Davies is saying something like this: If evolution confers capacities, even general capacities, that are roughly associated with some kind of direct utility, then we've got to explain how these same general capacities are far, far more powerful than any original use that could have produced them through some beneficial mutation. Both human and animal brains, in order to negotiate time and space, have a general capacity to recognize causal relationships. But only a human being uses this capacity to inquire into the similar material causes in the human and animal brain; asks about the question of causality as such, making the distinction between different kinds of causality; and spends long hours trying to discern the

2    Stephen Hawking, *A Brief History of Time*, 12–13.

causes and effects of things like black holes that have no relationship to everyday existence or any conceivable future utility.

Secondly, as we've noted, there is no necessary connection between natural selection and truth: a materially-determined brain state (whether we regard it as determined by physical laws or natural selection) is just that, a materially-determined brain state. Whereas evolution can account for useful ideas (be they true or false, or some mixture of the two), there is no essential connection between the brain state and reality that would cause true theories to appear in brain states, otherwise (to state the obvious), the history of science wouldn't be filled back to back with competing theories, many of which were outrageously wrong. The only connection that we could reasonably make is that certain beliefs prove to be helpful in regard to survival.

Here we must be especially careful not to allow someone like Dawkins to *assume* what he has to demonstrate or provide an inadequate demonstration. In making the case that evolution does explain the extraordinary level of intelligence that human beings have attained, we cannot allow some kind of anthropic hat-trick again such as this, "Well, you see that I just offered the proof, so the very fact that I offered the proof, shows that evolution must have given me sufficient intelligence! There, I've proven it!—and so God must not exist, since His intelligence would also have to be the product of evolution too." Perhaps Dawkins would do no such thing, and that would be to his credit.

We must be wary of another trick, the confusion of what is actually at issue. The question is not whether evolution has occurred, but whether Dawkins' purely reductionist anti-theistic account of evolution can explain human intelligence. One always has to watch a reductionist very carefully in this regard. If you say, "While your account of evolution does explain many things, I don't believe your account of evolution adequately explains human intelligence," he will likely hear, "I don't believe evolution explains anything at all." But to disagree about some things is not to disagree about everything. This is a point well-worth dwelling on, because it takes us, in a rather winding way, to the intellectual heart of Dawkins and his atheism.

If we might divert our discussion to Marxism for a moment, it might help us understand things more clearly. "Does it require deep intuition to comprehend that man's ideas, views, and conceptions, in one word, man's consciousness, change with every change in the condition of his material existence, in his social relations, and in his social life?" So ask Marx and Engels rhetorically in their *Manifesto of the Communist Party*.[3] Their philosophical argument which purportedly proved this contentious thesis was that, since the provision of food, clothing, and shelter is fundamental to all human beings, then everything about human life, including "man's ideas, views, and conceptions, in one word, man's consciousness," is merely a reflection of a particular society's way of producing these fundamental goods. You are what you eat, or more accurately, you are how you make what you eat.

Anyone with more than a passing knowledge of human nature would have to agree that providing for our material needs is fundamental to human beings everywhere, but only someone gone mad with ideological Marxism—and there have been many—would infer that everything about a society and everything about human nature, including all human thought, could be reduced to mere reflections of the economic modes of production of the particular society in which they occurred. Such madness violates another corollary of the above maxim: *Any philosophical account that makes the philosopher or his philosophy impossible is impossible as a philosophy.* To say the very least, if Marx were right, then his philosophy would be merely a reflection of the modes of produc-

---

3    Karl Marx and Friedrich Engels, *Manifesto of the Communist Party* in *Basic Writings on Politics and Philosophy*, edited by Lewis S. Feuer (Garden City, NY: Doubleday & Company, Inc., 1959), 26.

tion of his particular society. But since his thought is, like all thought, caused by the modes of production in his particular society, how would he know whether these were the right modes of production?

In taking issue with Marx, we would not reject the insightful things he has to say about the way that economic conditions often mold a particular people's social and intellectual culture, nor would we disregard the evils of industrialism he so poignantly described. We only cry foul when he tries to make a partial insight into an explanation of anything and everything.

In just the same way, to question whether Dawkins' version of natural selection *alone* can explain the immense capacities of the human mind, is not to deny that evolution has occurred or even that evolution is in very important ways a partial cause of human intelligence. As with Marx, we are only questioning whether the severely reductionist account of evolution offered by Dawkins, and that alone, can explain the advent of human intelligence. The evolution of human intelligence may not be a problem for some type of theistic account of evolution, but that is another issue. Our concern is not with a theistic account of evolution or even with a more robust, non-reductionist account of evolution, but with Dawkins' anti-theistic, purely reductionist account, because *that* is where he places all his argumentative bets.

As we've said in a previous chapter and repeated above, we believe that Dawkins fails to explain the advent of human intelligence because the capacity so far exceeds any credible relationship to survival or sexual attraction. The development of human intelligence cannot be correlated to any conceivable inch-by-million-year-inch climb up successive Mount Improbables given the exceedingly small time in which it would have to occur if it had occurred on Earth. The more "improbable" a thing, the more time it takes evolution to achieve it. Cells with a nucleus (eukaryotes) appeared 1.5 to 2 billion years ago. The first vertebrates appeared in the Cambrian explosion—biology's Big Bang—about 530,000,000 years ago. *Homo sapiens* arrived on the scene, perhaps, 130,000 to 250,000 years ago. On rough calculation, we're looking at a little over a half-billion years, which might seem like a lot, until we think how many miles up how many successive Mount Improbables evolution had to craw inch-by-million-year-inch to get from the simplest creatures with vertebrae to something able to think like Dawkins.

It is not enough, as Dawkins believes it is, merely to point out that other animals—crows, dolphins, chimpanzees—display quite complex, intelligent behavior because that only makes the problem worse. Now he's got to explain how *these* animals could evolve sufficient brain power to engage in their particular complex activities, and do so through successive random mutations in several different evolutionary branches—a bit like explaining why several different dealers independently dealt out perfect hands in bridge, since the odds of the successive mutations would amount to at least this level of improbability. But having done this, it would still not explain the enormous gap that exists between an animal using a stick to fish for termites and Michelangelo using a paintbrush on the ceiling of the Sistine Chapel or Shakespeare a quill pen to write *Hamlet*. The greater the power to be explained through its effect, the greater the number and height of the Mount Improbables that would have to be scaled. The only way to get around the problem is to take leap after leap, but as we've seen Dawkins himself admit, "Only God would essay the mad task of leaping up the precipice [of Mount Improbable] in a single bound."

None of this, we add, is a proof of God's existence, but an attempt to make clear that Dawkins has much more to explain, and the existence of the human intellect presents a formidable obstacle to his reductionist account. But there is another approach to demonstrating

God's existence—the argument from intelligibility—one that Dawkins never takes up.

This is not a short or easy argument because it depends on a significant amount of evidence from the latest findings in nearly all the sciences, from physics and astronomy, to chemistry and biology, and even more, from the history of science itself. In long form, the argument from intelligibility is contained in *A Meaningful World* (Benjamin Wiker and Jonathan Witt). It is the kind of approach that matches Pope Benedict's emphasis on the coincidence of the Divine *Logos*, or reason, in creation, and human *logos*, or reason, in science, and Christoph Cardinal Schönborn's emphasis on these very same themes.[4] It is also the kind of approach taken in the excellent book by astronomer Guillermo Gonzalez and philosopher Jay Richards, *The Privileged Planet: How our Place in the Cosmos is Designed for Discovery.*[5]

This is a scientific proof because it rests on the existence of the very activity of science itself. That science is even possible is something that needs to be explained. Let's assume the chance evolution of the human mind for a moment. If nature were indeed the result of chance, then it might happen that by chance, on some particular level, the evolved human mind could be able to make some intellectual headway in discovering the secrets of nature. But what we find—and what makes science possible as a successful, cumulative activity sustained over many centuries—is that nature is strangely amenable to rational inquiry on multiple, integrated levels, and especially on far more abstract levels than natural selection tied merely to survival or sexual selection could provide. Even

---

4   See Pope Benedict's Regensburg Address, "Faith, Reason, and the University," (September 12, 2006), available at the Vatican website: http://www.vatican.va/holy_father/benedict_xvi/speeches/2006/september/documents/hf_ben-xvi_spe_20060912_university-regensburg_en.html. And also Christoph Cardinal Schönborn, *Chance or Purpose? Creation, Evolution, and a Rational Faith* (San Francisco, CA: Ignatius, 2007), chaps. VII and IX.

5   Jay Richards, *The Privileged Planet: How our Place in the Cosmos is Designed for Discovery* (Washington, D.C.: Regnery Publishing, 2004).

stranger, nature seems to be designed tutorially, so that human beings are able to "read the book of nature" beginning with very simple concepts that bear unsuspected intellectual fruit, and which therefore allow for further discovery using more sophisticated concepts, and so on as scientists plumb its successive depths. This makes one suspicious not only that nature is intelligently written, but that it was written to be read by human beings with just the kind of capabilities they happen to have. In Pope Benedict's words, there is a profound "correspondence between our spirit and the prevailing rational structures of nature," a correspondence between mind and thing on every level of nature. That this correspondence is *given* in nature, and not contrived merely by human art, is what makes science a meaningful, successful activity.

Let us illustrate using mathematics. Mathematics is a human discipline; that is, we do not meet mathematical objects, like perfect circles or spheres, floating about in nature, nor do we happen across abstract concepts like the square root of two lying about like logs or leaves. Mathematical objects like circles and concepts like square roots are abstractions of the human mind. There may be two apples in front of us, but never two-ness. As the history of mathematics makes clear, while our mathematical beginnings (say, with the Egyptians or Babylonians) began with quite practical considerations, mathematics soon progressed with amazing rapidity into astoundingly beautiful but entirely abstract ruminations of no immediate discernible practical use. One need only work through that great monument of geometric and mathematical genius, the *Elements* of Euclid, written about three centuries before the birth of Christ, to witness this truth.

We'll use one quick example, perfect numbers. A perfect number is a positive integer that is the sum of its divisors (excluding itself). For example, 6 is a perfect number because you can add its divisors together and get 6 (that is, $1 + 2 + 3 = 6$). The next perfect number is 28 (because 1 + 2 + 4 + 7 + 14 = 28). There are, in fact, relative to the entire set of numbers, not very many perfect numbers at all (although, there may be an infinite number of them). The next one is 496, and after that, 8128. But then there's a big leap until you get to the fifth perfect number, 33,550,336. The next is 8,589,869,056. The entirely useless but intellectually intriguing task of defining and finding perfect numbers continues down to the present day, but even with all our computing powers and theoretical advances in mathematics, only a total of 39 perfect numbers have been found and verified. As the reader can guess, they get monstrously bigger and more difficult to find and verify.

The biggest perfect number known to the ancients was only 8128. But even so, Euclid was able to come up with the first significant proof to identify (not predict) *any* perfect number even though only four had been found so far. He demonstrates, in the most excruciatingly abstract way, that "if as many numbers as we please beginning from a unit be set out continuously in double proportion, until the sum of all becomes prime, and if the sum multiplied into the last make some number, the product will be perfect."[6] Perfectly amazing, perfectly abstract, but perfectly and elaborately useless.

Euclid's *Elements* is filled with many more examples of such wonderful mathematical and geometrical abstraction, none of which were directed to any practical use. To repeat, it would be exceedingly difficult to make a Darwinian case for the inch-by-million-year-inch slow climb up to an intellectual ability that so far exceeds any correlated benefit.

But that is not the main difficulty that faces an anti-theistic account of intellectual evolution, such as Dawkins'. The really strange thing is that Euclid's entirely abstract intellectual work became the foundation for the greatest advances in modern science precisely because there was a profound correlation between his geometrical and mathematical

---

6 Euclid, *Elements* (Heath translation), Book IX, Proposition 36.

methods of reasoning and nature itself. No one who has put Euclid's *Elements* and Isaac Newton's *Principia* (the full title of which is *Philosophiae Naturalis Principia Mathematica*) side by side can doubt that. The correlation between the *logos* of geometry and the *logos* of nature, between Euclid's geometry and the multitude of laws and relationships discovered by Newton, was so astounding that for at least three centuries afterward God was popularly recast as a Master Geometer. Even more interesting, the refinement of Newton's use of Euclid continued to lead to scientific discovery after scientific discovery, including the discovery of relativity that left Newton and Euclidean geometry behind for Einstein and non-Euclidean geometry. That is, the profound correlation between geometry and nature was not just on one level, but actually led to a multitude of scientific discoveries on many different levels in various scientific disciplines, from astronomy and physics to chemistry. This proved true in a rather interesting tutorial fashion. Obviously non-Euclidean geometry could not be discovered (or learned) before Euclidean geometry, and in fact it was developed in the early 1700s in response to a difficulty in Euclid concerning parallel lines. About three centuries later, non-Euclidean geometry replaced Euclidean geometry in physics, no one having foreseen such an application.

If nature had been randomly contrived, how could an originally abstract intellectual field of learning lead centuries later to countless scientific discoveries, the advances of which were made possible in great part by the prior advances in the purely intellectual mathematical disciplines? It can't be that the human mind happens to have evolved entirely abstract capabilities far exceeding any immediate benefit, and done so 2000 years prior to their application in understanding nature. Can nature itself just happened to have evolved millions of years earlier—billions, if we take it back to the beginning of the Big Bang—in such a way that its deeper, invisible structures and relationships prove, again and again, susceptible of mathematical articulation, the capacity for which was only evolved some thousands of years ago?

The problem is made all the more difficult because, as the history of science shows, we've gone far beyond Euclid in our development of mathematics, and the odd thing is, that once again, purely abstract mathematical constructions continue to prove fruitful in our analysis of nature.[7] The profound correlation between the human *logos* and the *logos* of nature continues; that is what gives life and hope to science.

On this we must add one final all-important point: the profound correlation between mathematics and nature is always ultimately defined according to nature; that is, the *logos* of nature is that by which any human mathematical construct is judged to be applicable. In short, the deep intelligibility of nature upon which science depends for its evident progress is a *given*. Here is the inference: in our experience, deep, multi-layered, and integrated intelligibility is always the result of a requisite intelligence. Dawkins' use of chance, on the other hand, is meant to displace the notion of intelligence. Things appear to be designed by an intelligence, he states, but random associations and mutations, and cumulative selection displace the need for intelligence as a cause. But here, we are not dealing with a biological entity that only "appears" to be intelligently designed in form and activity, and which can be an object of natural selection; we are dealing with the actual intelligibility of all nature that precedes and undergirds all biology. That is the starting point of science, the assumption of deep intelligibility, and it lies beyond Dawkins' account to explain it. Therefore, the existence of science would seem to demonstrate the existence of an Intelligent Creator.

We note here that one cannot avoid this theistic conclusion by saying, for example, that the laws of nature themselves (which have their own intrinsic mathematical intelligibility) caused the development in

7    For a more thorough analysis of this point, see Wiker and Witt, *Meaningful Universe*, chap. 4.

intelligence to be of such a kind that the mind matches the laws by which it is made. This is questionable on two counts.

First of all, the deep intelligibility expressed by the laws *is* what we are trying to explain. That there are laws at all, or more precisely, that nature is such that we can have progressive insights into its intelligible nature using very general mathematical principles and formulas—that is the strange thing that needs to be accounted for. The focus is on what is not subject to evolution and natural selection (nature, especially its intelligible but non-biological aspects) and not on what might have been involved in evolution (the human brain).

As for the second error, laws don't cause anything, so they can't act as a substitute for God. The all too common belief that laws do cause things is, as physicist Paul Davies rightly says, a new kind of Platonism where the laws of nature exist like Plato's ideas in some extra-natural realm, and somehow cause things to happen in our universe.[8] "In ortho-dox physics, the fact that nature conforms so efficiently to elegant math-ematical principles is left entirely unexplained. Physicists are obliged to assume the existence of two separate realms: the Platonic world of per-fect mathematical objects and relationships lying outside the physical universe and the world of space, time, and physical objects."[9] There is no such Platonic realm. Many physicists assume that there is such a realm because the alternative is (quite rightly) to realize that the mathematical intelligibility is written into *nature itself*, and we abstract the "laws" from nature through long, strenuous, but fruitful labor. The answer to the question, why does nature conform so efficiently to elegant mathemati-cal principles, is that nature is formed according to elegant mathemati-cal principles (or more exactly, nature is formed so that many aspects of its intelligibility can be represented by human mathematics).

---

8    Paul Davies, *Cosmic Jackpot*, chap. 10, pp. 235–242 (advance reading copy).
9    Paul Davies, *Cosmic Jackpot*, chap. 10, pp. 240–241.

Answering The New Atheism

Again, this would seem to defy a purely evolutionary explanation in two ways. The deep intelligibility of nature itself couldn't be caused by evolution because it precedes all biological evolution, and further, the extraordinary human capacity to grasp this deep intelligibility of nature as evidenced in modern science exceeds by far a reductionist account of the evolution of human intelligence. Since the activity of science does exist, we must have a non-reductionist explanation of human intelligence so we can account for it. To cling stubbornly to reductionism would therefore mean a violation of the above corollary and maxim: *Any theory in science that includes the existence of the scientist must allow both for the existence of the scientist and science itself*, and by implication, since Dawkins' proof of the improbability of God is based upon science, *Any demonstration of God's existence or non-existence must be of such a kind as to allow both for the existence of the demonstrator and for the possibility of demonstration.*

Given all this, we may also grasp a kind of proof (or at least an intimation) of the existence of God through beauty, something (as we said) Dawkins denied on a different level. Scientists have a very strong inclination to the beauty, or elegance of mathematical constructs. They attract the mind, even if they have no discernible practical value or theoretical value for science. It is very strange, indeed, then to find that the elegance of certain equations proves fruitful, and as it turns out, scientists are often inclined to choose the more elegant hypothetical constructs precisely because of their elegance.[10] The odd thing, of course, is that these elegant constructs often turn out to be the very ones that are most fruitful for the advance of science, as if nature itself tended toward the elegance. In this sense, beauty leads to truth, and

---

10 See Graham Farmelo, *It Must Be Beautiful: Great Equations of Modern Science* (London: Granta, 2002); Roberot Augros and George Stanciu, *The New Story of Science* (Lake Bluff, IL: Regnery, 1984), and Benjamin Wiker and Jonathan Witt, *A Meaningful World*, ch. 4.

since the truth is that nature is deeply intelligible, then we are back affirming the need for a Creative Intelligence.

5

# The Problem of Morality

## Grappling with Dawkins' Evolving Moral Universe

Rather than examine Dawkins' speculations about the evolutionary origins of religion, we are going directly to those on morality as they are more central and important to his entire argument. As the reader will see, religion will come up frequently. But Dawkins' account of the evolutionary origin of religion in the fifth chapter of *God Delusion* is seasoned with a heavy dose of vitriol and depends largely on his greatly contested account of "memes," "units of cultural inheritance," whose existence is predicated on analogy with genes. Repeating his splenetic outbursts in this chapter are not to his credit, and Dawkins' argument about memes is not worth considering, given that his theory of memes is so controversial even among his fellow non-believers. That having been said, we will take up any relevant points made in chapter five in our analysis of later chapters.

We must be very careful in approaching Dawkins' arguments about morality. First of all, they obviously don't exist in a vacuum, but are part of a rather long-standing debate in the West between atheists and Christians about whether atheists can be moral at all and, on the other side, whether Christianity leads to gross immoralities perpetrated in the name of faith. Unfortunately, the debate now often comes down to rather unproductive arguments about whether Hitler was an atheist or whether Nazism was just another form of Christian anti-Semitism. And so we have the tiresome *reductio ad Hitlerum* (which is all too often *argumentum ad infinitum* and hence *ad nauseam*). The atheist points backward to all the nasty things done by Christians in the Crusades, the Inquisition, the Thirty Years War, and takes these as premonitions of the atrocities of the Third Reich. Then, as a sign of the inherent goodness of atheists, he points to himself and other morally upright atheists. The theist points to the atrocities of Hitler, Stalin, and Mao as representative of atheism, and then to Mother Theresa of Calcutta as a sign of the inherent goodness of Christians. The atheist replies that, in fact, the crimes of Hitler were inspired by centuries of Christian anti-Semitism, and digs up some quotes showing Hitler's alleged Christian faith, and then finds quotes by atheists against fascism. The theist digs up some counter-quotes showing Hitler's alleged atheism, and then offers the lives of various devout Christians who smuggled Jews out of Germany as counter-evidence. The argument is endless.

In pointing out this frustration, we by no means wish to downplay the epic evil perpetrated by Hitler and the Nazis. If for no other reason, it provides a locus of agreement about evil between Christians and atheists, even when they disagree about so much else. That is why it plays so important a role in current debates about atheism and morality: it represents some common if unhallowed ground.

Given its importance, it is surprising that Dawkins devotes precious little space in his *God Delusion* to the Hitler question, addressing it only in a chapter subsection entitled "What About Hitler and Stalin? Weren't They Atheists?" In a more or less fair-minded but woefully short space, he concludes that Stalin was an atheist, but Hitler most likely wasn't. But anyway, it doesn't matter because "individual atheists may do evil things but they don't do evil things in the name of atheism." Of course, Stalin and Hitler did do very evil things, Dawkins admits, but in the name of something else (like Marxism, or "insane and unscientific eugenics theory tinged with sub-Wagnerian ravings"). By contrast, religious wars *are* done in the name of religion, and they occur throughout human history. Scratching his head, Dawkins reflects "I cannot think of any war that has been fought in the name of atheism. Why should it?...Why would anyone go to war for the sake of an *absence* of belief?"[1]

There are several odd things that should strike us about Dawkins' defense. To begin with, the statement that "individual atheists may do evil things but they don't do evil things in the name of atheism" is catchy but self-defeating. The obvious counter-statement would be that "individual Christians may do evil things but they don't do evil things in the name of Christianity." Each side would then be caught in an endless argument in regard to individual atheists and individual Christians, trying to sort through a tangled mass of evidence (much of which would be ambiguous) about the *real* motives of the individuals under consideration (much of which is impossible to retrieve). Whatever the ultimate merits of that exercise, we should at least see that it would be just as absurd to try to prove that *no* atheist *ever* did *anything* evil in the name of atheism, as it would be to try to prove that *no* Christian *ever* did *anything* evil in the name of Christianity. Christians must answer for the Inquisition, and atheists must answer for Stalin.

To avoid endless arguments and personal accusations, the debate should focus first and foremost on *principles*, not persons. As strange as it may sound, we should not judge atheism by passing judgment on individual atheists, nor should we judge Christianity by passing judgment on individual Christians. We should judge atheism by atheism, and Christianity by Christianity, each by its own principles. Then and only then will we be able to judge persons morally, atheists to see if they

1   Richard Dawkins, *The God Delusion*, 278.

are acting in accordance with atheism, Christians to see if they acting in accordance with Christianity.

There is another reason we should focus on principles. As Dawkins himself has just shown, blame can all too easily be diverted from one factor to another. It wasn't atheism that brought Hitler to do evil; it was "an insane and unscientific eugenics theory tinged with sub-Wagnerian ravings." (Or, in the case of Stalin, it wasn't atheism but "dogmatic and doctrinaire Marxism."[2]) We might also blame Hitler's morbid childhood, or the rise of Romantic German nationalism in the late 15th and early 16th centuries and its culmination in the 19th, or the humiliation of the Germans after World War I and the decrepit condition of the Weimar Republic. Since there are an indefinite number of conditions and pre-conditions for Hitler's rise, there are an indefinite number of ways to shift blame from the part played by atheism (if indeed it played any part). The same means to avoid blame for the Inquisition or the Thirty Years War could be used by Christians: the political aspirations of Spain in the late 15th century could be blamed for the Inquisition and the political machinations arising from the various nations vying for supremacy in the early 17th century could be justly cited as the real fundamental causes of the Thirty Years War.

In both cases, the blame is shifted from principles to various other contributing conditions. But what we really want to know is this: Is their something about the very principles of atheism that necessarily imply, lead to, or somehow entail certain immoral actions? Of course, the same question can and should be asked about the principles of Christianity.

That having been said, we cannot allow Dawkins his too easy dismissal of the fact that carnage on a level unknown in previous history occurred in the 20th century, and a significant amount of it was caused by regimes that counted themselves to be explicitly acting upon prin-

2   ibid.

ciples of atheism. Leaving aside the case of Hitler as ambiguous, the Soviet atheist regime purposely destroyed tens of millions of lives through mass executions, ideologically and politically motivated famines and warfare, and forced labor—some six to eight million under Lenin and twenty to twenty-five million under Stalin. At least this many are estimated to have been killed under Mao's communist regime, and a rough but conservative estimate of those slaughtered under the communist regimes in Eastern Europe, North Korea, Vietnam, Cambodia, and Cuba would be three million. "In brief," states Zbigniew Brzezinski, "the failed effort to build communism in the twentieth century consumed the lives of almost 60,000,000 human beings, making communism the most costly human failure in all of history."[3]

It is not enough to claim that the cause of these deaths was Marxist ideology and not atheism, because Marxism claimed to be a fulfillment of atheistic principles. If a similar death toll were attributable to Christian "ideology," it would demand more than such a casual explanation and avoidance of blame.

But perhaps even more important from our perspective is that atheism isn't merely the "absence of belief." To repeat Dawkins own words, "a universe with a creative superintendent would be a very different kind of universe from one without," and we add this all-important insight: *each kind of universe would entail a radically different notion of morality, as Dawkins himself demonstrates.* This is a fundamental point of our analysis that follows. Cosmology and morality are intimately related, and rival cosmological accounts imply rival views of morality. The reason for this is both simple and profound: different views of nature

---

3    Zbigniew Brzezinski, *Out of Control: Global Turmoil on the Eve of the 21ˢᵗ Century* (New York: Simon & Schuster, 1993), pp. 16–17. The figures are those calculated by Brzezinski in his chapter one, "The Century of Megadeath." His estimates are generally conservative. The estimates of the death toll do vary, a very good website offering a summary of them and their sources being http://users.erols.com/mwhite28/warstat1.htm.

imply different views of human nature, and different views of human nature will yield different moral principles.

We may therefore justly examine what kind of moral view is implied by Dawkins' evolutionary view of the universe. What we shall find will no doubt be disturbing to all sides in the debates concerning atheism, Christianity, and morality. Once we brush away surface similarities, we discover that *in principle* Christians and atheists inhabit different moral universes, where in great part what is good for the atheist is evil for the Christian, and what is evil for the atheist is good for the Christian. We stress "in principle" because in practice most atheists and Christians historically and culturally combine a confused mixture of moral principles, some of which can be traced backwards to Christian sources, some of which can be traced to secular sources that arose in antagonism to Christianity and culminate in atheism. Dawkins himself presents a very strange mixture.

That is all very abstract. So let us begin with a very concrete moral example, marriage, and, rather than use Dawkins, we shall return to his great predecessor, Charles Darwin. If a Christian husband cheats on his Christian wife, then he can be charged with adultery, and if he was a boaster of his own piety, with hypocrisy. But the charge of adultery and hypocrisy can only be made because of a particular moral principle (marriage is a life-long union between a man and a woman that excludes all extramarital sexual activity), which is itself rooted in nature (male and female unite sexually for procreation, a tenet of natural law) and in biblical revelation (Genesis 1:26–27, 2:18–25; Exodus 20:14; Deuteronomy 5:18; Matthew 19:3–9). This, of course, does not exclude the possibility that some other, non-Christian or pre-Christian cultures may not have had held monogamy up as a standard (the natural law, for instance, was expressed by the Roman Stoics), but only to point to the most important sources for the Christian cultural acceptance of monogamy as morally definitive. That having been said, most societies, including Jewish society, sanctioned polygamy, so Christian monogamy is exceptional.

We turn now to Charles Darwin's quite interesting book on the moral implications of his evolutionary theory, *The Descent of Man*. We must be clear that we are not examining Darwin's own life, but the moral principles and implications of evolutionary theory as he himself elucidated them. As far as we are aware, Darwin was every bit as upright as any Christian man in regard to his own marriage. He dearly loved his wife, Emma, and we're almost certain that he never committed adultery. But here are his rather startling words at the finale of the *Descent*.

> Man, like every other animal, has no doubt advanced to his present high condition through a struggle for existence consequent on his rapid multiplication; and if he is to advance still higher he must remain subject to a severe struggle. Otherwise he would soon sink into indolence, and the more highly-gifted men would not be more successful in the battle of life than the less gifted. Hence our natural rate of increase, though leading to many and obvious evils, must not be greatly diminished by any means. *There should be open competition for all men; and the most able should not be prevented by laws or customs from succeeding best and rearing the largest number of offspring.*[4]

The principle underlying these statements is, of course, the famous principle of natural selection that made its debut in Darwin's more famous *Origin of Species*, a principle that, as Darwin makes quite startlingly clear in the *Descent*, applies to human beings just as it does

---

4   Charles Darwin, *The Descent of Man, and Selection in Relation to Sex*, with an Introduction by John Tyler Bonner and Robert M. May (Princeton, NJ: Princeton University Press, 1981), pt. II, chap. XXI, p. 403. Emphasis added.

to all other animals. The engine of evolution is the natural selection of the most fit over the less fit in the struggle to survive. From this, one can derive a quasi-moral principle something like "the best should breed the most." But monogamous marriage is detrimental to this principle because it artificially restricts the breeding of the best (after all, no one would unite his champion racehorse to one and only one mare for life). Thus: *"There should be open competition for all men; and the most able should not be prevented by laws or customs from succeeding best and rearing the largest number of offspring."*

We do not know what Darwin's wife Emma thought of this suggestion, nor if she ever read it, but there is no getting around the inference that the "laws or customs" Darwin regards as obstacles have to do with monogamy. If he is not condoning adultery, he is at least nudging toward polygamy, but these are only "bad" according to the tenets of Christianity. We see clearly the clash of rival moral views: what is morally bad according to the Christian (adultery or polygamy) can be morally good according to the Darwinian.

To be more exact, whether or not Darwin himself was a Christian, if we accept evolution and *subtract* the particular moral claims made about marriage that are historically due to Christian influence (that is, if we cancel Christianity by accepting atheism), then restricting sexuality to male-female, life-long monogamy is senseless if not downright pernicious. If such is the case, we might charge Darwin with being a hypocrite for *not* committing adultery. In saying this, we are not saying that Darwinism leads to sexual libertinism, but that according to the fundamental principles of evolution, restriction of the sexual activity of the "best" by the entirely artificial and religiously-based confines of monogamy goes directly *against* the principles of non-theistic evolution.

Anyone who has read Dawkins realizes why this example is so important. Dawkins is *the* world spokesman for the atheistic form of evolution. He quite clearly embraces an anti-theistic evolution as a kind of counter-philosophy that displaces the need for God as creator of the cosmos. In making this point clear, we do not at all mean to say that to embrace evolution in any and every form leads directly to atheism, only that those who embrace atheism necessarily embrace evolution as a counter-philosophy to divine creation *and* reject any theistic principles that would qualify it. This has moral implications: an atheist cannot affirm a godless account of evolution *and* a kind of sexual fidelity that is historically peculiar to Christianity.

Now that we've had a particular illustration, we may look at the grand scale of things again. But there is one aspect that must remain very particular, the comparison of Christianity with the kind of atheism espoused by Dawkins. We cannot engage in a comparison of the most general forms of religion and atheism because no such merely general forms exist, and the particular forms differ considerably. Hinduism and Christianity are religions, but they set out very different views of the cosmos, and therefore inhabit entirely different moral universes. To take the most obvious instance, the caste system of Hinduism is the result of their belief in reincarnation. But Christians do not believe in a universe in which a person is punished for sins by being continually reincarnated in lower societal castes, and then into lower life forms. In regard to atheism, we encounter similar divergences. The ancient Greek atheist Epicurus was an ascetic, and therefore focused on self-control, whereas the modern atheist Friedrich Nietzsche, in some ways ascetic, extolled the will to power. With Dawkins it is more complicated, since he presents a not always very coherent mixture of aspects of modern secular liberalism with evolutionary theory. So again, even while look-ing at the grand scale of things, we shall have to be particular as well, comparing Christianity with the kind of atheism Dawkins holds. Doing so will ultimately help us sort out and evaluate his moral case against Christianity in *The God Delusion*.

What, then, is good and evil for Richard Dawkins? In *River Out of Eden: A Darwinian View of Life* Dawkins famously states that "nature is not cruel, only pitilessly indifferent. This is one of the hardest lessons for humans to learn. We cannot admit that things might be neither good nor evil, neither cruel nor kind, but simply callous—indifferent to all suffering, lacking all purpose."[5] A universe without God, as Dawkins understands it, *is* a universe without moral purpose.

This is not a new position. The great 17th century atheist Thomas Hobbes (the founder of modern secular liberalism) understood this just as clearly. For Hobbes, nature is just matter in motion, and consequently nature is neither moral nor immoral, but *a*moral. There is no intrinsic good or evil for the very reason we don't speak about good and evil combinations of the chemical elements: the chemical elements just *are*; their combinations happen by necessity and fortuity.

Since according to this materialistic view, larger things are merely the sum of their material parts, then larger things are amoral as well. A particular oak tree is not moral or immoral in its growing upward and crowding out a neighboring maple. It just *is* or, more accurately, the oak tree just does what its material constituents make it do. A victorious male lion that has just vanquished a fellow male of the pride is neither moral nor immoral in eating the cubs of the previous king. He is just being a male lion. Finally, human beings are neither moral nor immoral by nature, for in our natural state there is no such thing as good and evil. As Hobbes makes clear in his classic of modern political philosophy *Leviathan*, the distinctions "good" and "evil" are merely projections of human desires and aversions.

---

5   Richard Dawkins, *River Out of Eden: A Darwinian View of Life* (New York: Basic Books, 1995), 95–96

> That which men Desire, they are also sayd to LOVE: and to HATE those things, for which they have Aversion….But whatsoever is the object of any mans Appetite or Desire; that is it, which he for his part calleth *Good*: And the object of his Hate, and Aversions, *Evill*; And of his Contempt, *Vile* and *Inconsiderable*. For these words of Good, Evill, and Contemptible, are ever used with relation to the person that useth them: There being nothing simply and absolutely so; nor any common Rule of Good and Evill, to be taken from the nature of the objects themselves.[6]

All of this follows for Hobbes precisely because human desires are merely the result of material actions and reactions, attraction and repulsion on the atomic level, far below the level of human awareness. Human individuals, as conglomerations of atoms, are attracted and repulsed by things that please and pain them, which they *call* good and evil respectively, even though there is "nothing simply and absolutely so; nor any common Rule of Good and Evill, to be taken from the nature of the objects themselves."

The German philosopher Friedrich Nietzsche, writing three centuries later, likewise argued that a godless universe entails a rejection of any notion of good and evil except as human-made subjective projections onto an indifferent, if not hostile, cosmos. Chiding the ancient (and modern) Stoics for holding the view that intrinsic moral guidelines are written into nature, Nietzsche (sounding almost exactly like Dawkins) scoffs:

---

6   Thomas Hobbes, *Hobbes's Leviathan*, reprint of the 1651 edition of *Leviathan, or The Matter, Forme, & Power of a Common-wealth Ecclesiasticall and Civill* (Oxford: Clarendon Press, 1965), I.6, pp. 39–41 [23–24]. See also I.15, p. 122–123 [79–80].

> "According to nature" you want to *live*? O you noble
> Stoics, what deceptive words these are! Imagine a
> being like nature, wasteful beyond measure, indif-
> ferent beyond measure, without purposes and con-
> sideration, without mercy and justice, fertile and
> desolate and uncertain at the same time; imagine
> indifference itself as a power—how *could* you live
> according to this indifference?[7]

Nietzsche, *the* greatest philosopher of modern atheism, is important for our consideration, since he was the philosopher at the foundation of the so-called "Wagnerian ravings" of the Nazis. Moreover, in
his *Beyond Good and Evil*, Nietzsche provides an extension of Darwin's
account of morality that sounds strikingly like Hitler's and which, in a
popularized form, provided the foundation for Nazism.

Richard Dawkins is no follower of Nietzsche or the Nazis, but
he's got to make clear how he can take the same amoral foundations of
nature and embrace Darwinism but not lead to a similar moral view.
The difficulties that he faces can best be understood by going back to
Darwin to see how he himself treated morality, a task that shall take the
rest of this chapter.

For Darwin, everything needs an evolutionary explanation, including morality. In his famous *Origin of Species*, he offered the evolutionary explanation that would provide the founding principle of his
approach to biology:

> As many more individuals of each species are born
> than can possibly survive; and as, consequently,
> there is a frequently recurring struggle for existence,
> it follows that any being, if it vary however slightly

---

7    Friedrich Nietzsche, *Beyond Good and Evil*, translated by Walter Kaufmann (New York: Vin-
     tage, 1966), section 9.

in any manner profitable to itself, under the complex and sometimes varying conditions of life, will have a better chance of surviving, and thus be *naturally selected*. From the strong principle of inheritance, any selected variety will tend to propagate its new and modified form.[8]

But how does this relate to morality? For Darwin (as for Hobbes, Nietzsche, and Dawkins as well), morality is not itself natural; there is no natural good and evil. Rather, what we *call* morality is one of the effects of the natural selection of traits that, for some reason or other, contributed directly or indirectly to survival in the struggle of life. This is such an important point to dwell upon because it so severely damages Dawkins' moral case against Christianity and his own attempt to transcend the morality of Darwinism.

As Darwin boldly claims, no one else has yet approached morality "exclusively from the side of natural history."[9] A natural *history* of morality traces its evolutionary development, not only in regard to how it arose, but (along with every other evolved trait like coloration or beak shape or type of eye) how it varied and continues to vary as conditions change.

Note that neither the evolutionary process nor the results are themselves moral. Natural selection itself is *pre*-moral and the result (some particular "moral" trait) is not *itself* moral according to an objective, eternal, or immutable standard any more than a particular shape of a bird's beak is good or evil. A particular shape for a bird's beak is good for *this* kind of bird, under *these* conditions, pertaining at *this* historical time. But a duck's bill, while good for the duck, is not good for the eagle. And even for the duck, if conditions change, that particular shape may actually prove detrimental or not as fit as some modification. The same

8 Charles Darwin, *The Origin of Species* (New York: Mentor, 1958), "Introduction," p. 29.
9 Charles Darwin, *The Descent of Man*, pt. I, chap. III, p. 71.

is true for every kind of trait, including those that we would call "moral." So, when we say "good for" or "bad for" in regard to evolution we must remember that these are not moral terms. For this reason, there cannot be intrinsically evil actions among animals, and human beings are one more kind of animal.

To use an example from Dawkins, cannibalism among animals is rare, not because cannibalism is evil, but because it is a bad evolutionary strategy. "Members of one's own species are made of meat too. Why is cannibalism relatively rare?...The reason [for example] that lions do not hunt lions is that it would not be an ESS [Evolutionarily Stable Strategy] for them to do so. A cannibal strategy would be unstable [because there]...is too much danger of retaliation."[10]

To explain, an ESS is "a strategy which, if most members of a population adopt it, cannot be bettered by an alternative strategy."[10] Cannibalism is a bad strategy for an entire population for the obvious reason that, if the "cannibal" trait spread throughout a population of (say) lions, they would be eaten up or severely beaten up by their own strategy in short order.

An important takeaway lesson here is that for Dawkins, if he follows the logic of Darwinism, cannibalism isn't evil even for human beings. It's just a bad strategy. Of course, it would be an Evolutionarily Stable Strategy for a particular group of human beings if they simply ate human beings from other tribes or races, and we do find quite stable societies that have adopted cannibalism. If human beings are simply one more kind of animal generated by evolution, then such cannibalism cannot be condemned.

This brings us back to the problem of relativism, and that of a particular kind. We can now see why on a purely evolutionary account of morality there would be many different kinds of moralities and not

---

10  Richard Dawkins, The Selfish Gene, p. 83.

just one morality for all humanity. That does not mean "anything goes," but anything goes that contributes to survival under particular conditions. Moral traits, like all traits, are naturally selected as more fit under particular conditions for particular peoples, conditions that do not pertain for other peoples. There is no independent standard of morality. Even in regard to one people, when conditions under which the original "moral" traits were selected change, different "moral" traits will be selected. That is why Darwin has to provide a natural history of morality. As with every other trait subject to evolutionary change, moralities come and go, branch off and diverge.

From where do they come? For Darwin, the "moral sense" develops *after* the "social sense," and this development is not specifically human: "any animal whatever, endowed with well-marked social instincts, would inevitably acquire a moral sense or conscience as soon as its intellectual powers had become as well developed, or nearly as well developed, as in man."[11] Not the *same* moral sense, but one that serves the particular fitness of the animal. Darwin uses the imaginative example of "men…reared under precisely the same conditions as hive-bees," wherein the "unmarried females would, like the worker-bees, think it a sacred duty to kill their brothers, and mothers would strive to kill their fertile daughters; and no one would think of interfering." They would be governed by the conscience appropriate to hive-bees, "an inward monitor," but this inner voice would nag them to commit fratricide and infanticide.[12]

We needn't dwell on merely imaginary cases. We have already seen that while the necessity of breeding is obviously essential for human evolution, there is no particular mode of marriage that is essentially moral according to evolution. Monogamous marriage *may*

---

11  Charles Darwin, *The Descent of Man*, pt. I, chap. III, pp. 71–72.
12  Charles Darwin, *The Descent of Man*, pt. I, chap. III, p. 73.

have somehow contributed to the fitness of some particular people at some particular time under some particular conditions, but that would have been exceptional. That is, since natural selection itself runs at peak performance the more offspring there are from the more fit, then it follows that monogamy would be a strange exception in the natural history of morality. Monogamy isn't a standard. It is something that a good evolutionist like Darwin or Dawkins tries to *explain* as an exception, not something that evolution itself tries to *achieve* as a natural or moral goal.

We also are not talking about just the "nice" moral traits, as might be implied by Dawkins' evolutionary explanation of altruism through genetic kinship, reciprocity, and so on.[13] Dawkins cannot gloss over the "cruelty" that might contribute to the survival of some particular species or group of human beings. As Darwin noted, some animals "will expel a wounded animal from the herd, or gore or worry it to death," which Darwin oddly calls "almost the blackest fact in natural history," but which nonetheless can be explained as contributing to the survival of a particular evolutionary population. This has interesting ramifications, as Darwin points out, for animals harrying to death the wounded of their own kind "is not much worse than that of the North American Indians who leave their feeble comrades to perish on the plains, or the Feegeans, who, when their parents get old or fall ill, bury them alive."[14] There is this difference: since leaving feeble comrades to die and burying old parents contributes to the survival of the Indians and Feegeans, then like the fictional honey-bee men, these actions are *moral* for each respectively.

This brings up another startling truth. Even the evolution of such seemingly universal moral "commands" as "Do not steal" and "Do not

13  Richard Dawkins, *The God Delusion*, 219–222.
14  Charles Darwin, *The Descent of Man*, pt. I, chap. III, pp. 76–77.

murder" are not actually universal. They evolve as moral traits relative to particular tribes *because* that is the only place that the natural selection of moral traits can occur. The evolutionary version of the command is "Thou shalt not kill *any of us.*" Darwin is well-worth quoting at length in this regard.

> The virtues which must be practiced, at least generally, by rude men, so that they may associate in a body, are those which are still recognized as the most important. But they are practiced almost exclusively in relation to the men of the same tribe; and their opposites are not regarded as crimes in relation to the men of other tribes. No tribe could hold together if murder, robbery, treachery, &c., were common; consequently such crimes within the limits of the same tribe "are branded with everlasting infamy:" but excite no such sentiment beyond these limits. A North-American Indian is well pleased with himself, and is honoured by others, when he scalps a man of another tribe; and a Dyak cuts off the head of an unoffending person and dries it as a trophy. The murder of infants has prevailed on the largest scale throughout the world, and has met with no approach; but infanticide, especially of females, has been thought to be good for the tribe, or at least not injurious. Suicide during former times was not generally considered a crime, but rather from the courage displayed as an honourable act; and it is still largely practised by some semi-civilised nations without reproach, for the loss to a nation of a single individual is not felt....It has been recorded that an Indian Thug conscientiously regretted that he had not strangled and robbed as many travelers as did his father before him. In a rude state of civilisation the robbery of strangers is, indeed, generally considered as honourable.

> The great sin of Slavery has been almost universal, and
> slaves have often been treated in an infamous manner.
> As barbarians do not regard the opinion of their wom-
> en, wives are commonly treated like slaves. Most sav-
> ages are utterly indifferent to the sufferings of strang-
> ers, or even delight in witnessing them.[15]

To say the least, it is interesting that Darwin called slavery a "great sin," given that its very universality attests to its evolutionary usefulness. In fact, Darwin could not condemn any of these actions on principle (even though he did in practice). As we have seen, in accord with his account of the evolution of morality, there is no objective, independent morality by which they can be condemned. Since morality itself is defined by traits that contribute to the survival of particular peoples at particular times, any such trait listed above that contributes to the survival of some particular people is moral, by definition, *for that people*. Natural selection itself is not subject to morality. It is the amoral foundation of the social instinct that is in turn the foundation of all moralities. Therefore, nothing that allows the fit to survive can be considered immoral. (We'll see how this pertains to his analysis of the Bible later on.) The core of the difficulty for Darwinism, especially for Dawkins' antitheistic version, is again that human beings are classed as just one among a large number of species of animals. As a consequence, Darwinism must treat human beings and animals on the same plane, which means that *evolved moral traits can only be explained, not condoned or condemned*. A female praying mantis bites off and eats the head of the male during mating. The task of Darwin or Dawkins is not one of moral remonstrance and possible rehabilitation of the offending cannibal, but to search for a reason for such macabre mating in terms of natural selection as to how such cannibalism has either proximately or remotely ben-

---

15 Charles Darwin, *The Descent of Man*, pt. I, chap. III, pp. 93–94.

efited—been "good for"—praying mantises. The same task, explanation not condemnation, faces Darwinism in regard to human cannibalism, infanticide, burying one's parents alive, genocidal warfare, and so on. On the other end of things, giving an evolutionary explanation for the appearance of altruism, does not mean that altruism is somehow better or an evolutionary goal.

The problems don't end there. Both Darwin and Dawkins, for their own respective reasons, define some evolved moral traits as (ironically) more moral or at least more desirable than others. This itself is not possible on evolutionary grounds. But even beyond that, it is worth noting another, rather interesting difficulty: any later desirable moral trait depended upon some earlier undesirable moral trait for its development. The development from higher animals to someone like Darwin or Dawkins necessarily had to go through the "savage" stage: there is no way to get to the well-mannered, liberal, cosmopolitan Englishman except through the barbarian. As Darwin himself drilled in, *Natura non facit saltum*,[16] "Nature does not make a leap," and that is as true for moral qualities as it is for physical or intellectual qualities. Therefore, whatever moral qualities Darwin or later Dawkins fancies himself having, these qualities are actually historically and evolutionarily dependent on the above-described qualities of savages.

This is a telling point. Darwin attempts to posit a certain kind of morality, or more accurately, a particular moral trait, sympathy, as the evolutionary peak. (Dawkins makes a similar move, as we'll soon see, in regard to altruism.) Sympathy is the ability to feel, by imagination, the sufferings of another, and this brings us "to relieve the sufferings of another, in order that our own painful feelings may be at the same time relieved."[17] "As man advances in civilisation," Darwin

16   Charles Darwin, *The Origin of Species*, chap. VII, "Special Difficulties," p. 184.
17   Charles Darwin, *The Descent of Man*, pt. I, chap. III, p. 81.

asserts, "the simplest reason would tell each individual that he ought to extend his social instincts and sympathies to all the members of the same nation, though personally unknown to him. This point being once reached, there is only an artificial barrier to prevent his sympathies extending to the men of all nations and races." And it doesn't stop there: "Sympathy beyond the confines of man, that is humanity to the lower animals, seems to be one of the latest moral acquisitions," so that in the evolutionary march morally upward and outward, "our sympathies becoming more tender and more widely diffused," finally becoming "extended to all sentient beings."[18]

Even if we accept the notion of evolution's upward moral climb (which is highly dubious), Darwin would have to admit that for 99% of the natural history of morality, the decidedly unsympathetic savagery described in the paragraphs above pertained *and* formed the evolutionary scaffold upon which the development of sympathy *had* to evolve.

But having said all this, we realize that we cannot accept the notion of "upward moral climb." Perhaps Darwin might still have had some whiff of theism in his soul, but Dawkins does not, and as all non-starry-eyed evolutionists admit, evolution doesn't aim upward. It doesn't aim anywhere. There is no up or down to evolution; there is just survival of the fittest, and that is the only standard by which evolution judges better or worse. On evolutionary grounds, "more moral" can only mean "contributing somehow to better survival of this particular group under these particular conditions."

A sign of Darwin's fundamental confusion is that the evolved trait of sympathy could very well conflict directly with the survival of the fittest, in which case so much the worse for sympathy and so much the better for savagery. Ironically, we find the conflict expressed by Darwin himself. As he himself notes:

18 Charles Darwin, *The Descent of Man*, pt. I, chap. III, pp. 100–101.

With savages, the weak in body or mind are soon eliminated; and those that survive commonly exhibit a vigorous state of health. We civilised men, on the other hand, do our utmost to check the process of elimination; we build asylums for the imbecile, the maimed, and the sick; we institute poor-laws; and our medical men exert their utmost skill to save the life of every one to the last moment. There is reason to believe that vaccination has preserved thousands, who from a weak constitution would formerly have succumbed to small-pox. Thus the weak members of civilised societies propagate their kind. No one who has attended to the breeding of domestic animals will doubt that this must be highly injurious to the race of man. It is surprising how soon a want of care, or care wrongly directed, leads to the degeneration of a domestic race; but excepting in the case of man himself, hardly any one is so ignorant as to allow his worst animals to breed.[19]

But, warns Darwin, we must resist the temptation to embrace natural selection at the expense of the evolved trait of sympathy. "Nor could we check our sympathy, if so urged by hard reason, without deterioration in the noblest part of our nature...[for] if we were intentionally to neglect the weak and helpless, it could only be for a contingent benefit, with a certain and great present evil. Hence we must bear without complaining the undoubtedly bad effects of the weak surviving and propagating their kind." The most we can do, if we wish to salvage sympathy from savagery, is somehow to ensure that "the weaker and inferior members of society [are] not marrying so freely as the sound" which can occur "by the weak in body or mind refraining from marriage."[20]

---

19  Charles Darwin, *The Descent of Man*, pt. I, chap. V, p. 168.
20  Charles Darwin, *The Descent of Man*, pt. I, chap. V, p. 169.

Hence the conflict. On the one hand Darwin urges the reader to harsh eugenic conclusions through a strict application of natural selection and then pulls him back, softening his hard eugenic conclusions out of his desire to retain the evolved moral trait of sympathy. The difficulties of this position should be obvious. Why *not* follow hard reason, since hard reason follows evolution? Evolution is the very foundation of the moral trait of sympathy, but evolution favors sympathy or any trait *only insofar* as it contributes to survival. Why keep it when there is a conflict? Or more exactly, natural selection will itself eliminate those who rely on sympathy when savagery would bring about survival. Even more embarrassing, on his own grounds Darwin's confession that sympathy is the highest evolved moral trait is merely a description of his own evolved feelings. They are no more superior to other evolved feelings as evolutionary traits than, say, the shape of his head or the color of his hair.

It is not difficult to see that hard reason could lead all too easily to the kind of eugenic conclusions espoused by the Nazis, something that both Darwin in prospect and Dawkins in retrospect would count as abominable. But again, our focus is on principles and not persons.

The difficulty is all the more severe given the way that racial struggle among humans was counted by Darwin as essential to human evolutionary advance. For Darwin, the distinct human races are the result of natural selection working amidst the "struggle for existence," so that as with many other species, quite distinct "races" evolve, "some of which are so different that they have often been ranked by naturalists as distinct species"[21] (although Darwin preferred to think of the different races as "sub-species"[22]). Quite naturally, the struggle for existence takes place as the struggle *between* races, that is, between the closest evolu-

---

21 Charles Darwin, *The Descent of Man*, pt. I, chap. VI, p. 185.
22 Charles Darwin, *The Descent of Man*, pt. I, chap. VII, p. 235.

tionary rivals, so that "extinction follows chiefly from the competition of tribe with tribe, and race with race."[23] Of course, the extinction that follows the struggle to survive *is* natural selection at work, that is *how* the fittest tribes or races (with their respective traits) are selected and the less fit eliminated. Since the struggle to survive works incessantly, such racial antagonism must continue, which is why Darwin can simply describe the future extermination of particular races with evident scientific detachment.

> At some future period, not very distant as measured by centuries, the civilised races of man will almost certainly exterminate and replace throughout the world the savage races. At the same time the anthropomorphous apes [i.e., most human-looking, like the gorilla or chimpanzee] will no doubt be exterminated. The break [i.e., the evolutionary gap] will then be rendered wider, for it will intervene between man in a more civilised state…than the Caucasian, and some ape as low as a baboon, instead of as at present between the negro or Australian and the gorilla.[24]

If this doesn't send a cold shudder down one's spine, then what could? We wager it sends a shudder down Dawkins' spine as well, and that is to his credit. But that having been said, he clearly must come up with another reason outside of evolution, it would seem, by which he could condemn racial antagonism and extinction.

The same holds for war. Again, Dawkins rather glibly stated, "I cannot think of any war that has been fought in the name of atheism. Why should it?…Why would anyone go to war for the sake of an *absence* of belief?" Even laying aside the obvious counter-instances of ex-

23 Charles Darwin, *The Descent of Man*, pt. I, chap. VII, p. 238.
24 Charles Darwin, *The Descent of Man*, pt. I, chap. VI, p. 201.

ternal and internal wars fought by communists, we can see that, given an anti-theistic account of evolution, that is, one that occurs in the *absence* of belief, wars cannot be condemned because they are one of the most effective modes of natural selection. This is a point Darwin himself made (ironically, at least for Dawkins' complaint) in his discussion of the evolutionary development of *moral* qualities, i.e., the development of morality depends upon war, therefore such wars cannot be immoral.

> When two tribes of primeval man, living in the same country, came into competition, if the one tribe includ-ed...a greater number of courageous, sympathetic, and faithful members,...this tribe would succeed best and conquer the other. Let it be borne in mind how all-important, in the never-ceasing wars of savages, fidelity and courage must be. The advantage which disciplined soldiers have over undisciplined hordes follows chiefly from the confidence which each man feels in his com-rades....Selfish and contentious people will not co-here, and without coherence nothing can be effected. A tribe possessing the above qualities in a high degree would spread and be victorious over other tribes; but in the course of time it would, judging from all past history, be in its turn overcome by some other and still more highly endowed tribe. Thus the social and moral qualities would tend slowly to advance and be diffused throughout the world.[25]

That does not mean, of course, that World War II should be blamed solely upon the inflammation of Germans by Darwinian be-liefs and rhetoric—although Darwinism must shoulder its share of the blame—but that from a Darwinian perspective, war (like morality) is something to be explained, something that is (to use Dawkins' words)

---

25 Charles Darwin, *The Descent of Man*, pt. I, chap. V, pp. 162–163.

"horribly frequent in history," and hence which must have an evolutionary explanation in terms of some benefit. Darwin gave it one. We might note that Darwin's affirmation of war as an essential aspect of human evolution in his *Descent* is mirrored in his presentation in the *Origin of Species* of the struggle for existence in all nature as a kind of war, speaking of the "great battle of life,"[26] and the "war of nature."[27] To all this we add that Dawkins' subtraction of a supernatural source of morality makes it doubly hard to condemn war as violating some objective moral standard. In sum, war itself doesn't violate the principle of natural selection; it illustrates it admirably.

Given all this we can now see why it is that Richard Dawkins, the arch-evolutionist, actually *denies* that evolution should be our moral gauge, even while he affirms that all moral traits somehow must be derived from evolution. This is such an important point that he has repeated it several times. In his *Selfish Gene* he informs the reader that "I am not advocating a morality based on evolution," and indeed, "Be warned that if you wish, as I do, to build a society in which individuals cooperate generously and unselfishly towards a common good, you can expect little help from biological nature. Let us try to *teach* generosity and altruism, because we are born selfish."[28] In fact, it would seem that Dawkins himself largely agrees that strictly following Darwinism would lead to something like Hitler. As he stated in an interview, "No decent person wants to live in a society which works according to Darwinian laws....A Darwinian society would be a Fascist state."[29]

But that leaves him in a very strange and paradoxical position. Dawkins' account of morality cannot ultimately come from nature be-

26 Charles Darwin, *The Origin of Species*, chap. III, "Struggle for life," p. 86.
27 Charles Darwin, *The Origin of Species*, chap. III, "Struggle for life," p. 87.
28 Richard Dawkins, *The Selfish Gene*, 2–3.
29 From an interview in the Austrian daily paper, *Die Presse* (July 30, 2005, p. 8), as quoted in Christoph Cardinal Schönborn, *Chance or Purpose? Creation, Evolution, and a Rational Faith*, translated by Henry Taylor (San Francisco: Ignatius, 2007), 170.

cause nature really is "red in tooth and claw" (which, Dawkins elsewhere notes, "sums up our modern understanding of evolution admirably"[30]). Yet, morality cannot have a *super*natural source either, since he's a devout atheist. One might well wonder what other possible source there *could* be? For our purposes, this is no small question because a significant part of his case against Christianity is the moral case. If Christianity is immoral, then it has to be immoral according to *something*. We'll try to sort out what in the next chapter.

To conclude our current chapter, we've slowly uncovered the differences between the Christian moral universe and the Darwinian moral universe. We must now make things more clear by way of a summary. At the very foundation of Christian morality is the Judeo-Christian assumption that human beings are fundamentally distinct from animals. While human beings are in important respects animals, since they are made in the image of God, they become the locus of certain definite moral standards, standards that are clarified by revelation. It doesn't matter in the least that other animals engage in various acts that contribute to their survival—infanticide, cannibalism, incest, savagery toward the sick and injured—because human beings are not merely animals but special creatures whose lives are made sacred by the Creator.

Divine commands, then, are rooted in nature (and here we are taking a Catholic natural law position, where God's moral commands are expressed through nature, not by arbitrary fiat). To use an obvious example, "Do not murder" is a command that pertains to human beings alone *because* they are human beings. It does not mean "Do not kill lions, goats, fish, etc." As another example, marriage is a certain kind of sacred institution that is rooted in the animal distinction of male and female but goes far beyond it, to include a kind of fidelity defined by the Creator rather than by mere procreation. These kinds

30 Richard Dawkins, *The Selfish Gene*, 2.

of commands are considered inviolable because they are rooted in human nature as defined by its being in the image of God; that is, human beings share in God's own sacred inviolability. Moral good and evil, then, are rooted in created nature.

For the Darwinian universe, absent any Creator, the human species is a transient production of impersonal causes that are part of an entirely amoral understanding of nature. Since the various moralities are simply sets of traits produced by evolution that have no more permanence than the conditions which created them, then there can be no single standard of morality. Some societies may find some moral traits that are both compatible to Christian moral traits and happen to be beneficial for them, but others may find that such Christian-compatible moral traits hinder their survival. In either case, the only issue is whether some trait contributes to survival; no action can be condemned as intrinsically evil. The question is: Does it promote survival? If it does, it is "good." If it brings self-destruction, the trait isn't morally evil, but (at best) bad evolutionary strategy.

# 6

# DAWKINS' MORALITY

## Dawkins' Gospel of Super Niceness

As we've just seen, Dawkins himself seems to repudiate the moral implications of evolutionary theory. True to his claim that there is no good or evil in nature, he also asserts that we cannot derive any moral guidance from evolution, and in fact, if we let the brutalities of natural selection be our moral and societal guide, we would end up creating an "immoral" society.

But then where and how *does* Dawkins ground morality? With what we've seen so far, he appears to have placed himself in a difficult situation. He posits an amoral universe—one without intrinsic good and evil—precisely because no God exists. But if Dawkins wants to condemn Christians for immorality—*really* wants to condemn them—then it would seem that he must accept a moral universe, which would in turn demand a deity (since the lack of a deity is what characterizes it as amoral).

Providing an evolutionary account of morality does not help his case either. As we have seen, the principle of natural selection is fundamental and amoral, and morality is simply one more thing that must be explained by evolution. He can give an account of the evolutionary rise of various moral traits, but these traits themselves aren't morally better or worse. They are simply the traits that helped particular peoples survive. The result is that on his own principles, Dawkins can only explain but never condemn. The point of an evolutionist is not to condemn the carnage of war throughout history, but to explain its continual occurrence in human history in terms of its contribution to the survival of the fittest. Making things more difficult, at least two of the most infamous crimes of Nazism—eugenics and racial extermination—appear to follow directly from the principles of natural selection. The difficulty is even more acute for Dawkins because, as Darwin made clear, the struggle for survival between races—and the consequent racial extermination—is the very mode by which human evolution has progressed. Yet, we know that Dawkins does want to condemn these things. But on his own account, "to condemn" would mean at the very best "to make others aware that such things conflict with my evolved moral traits."

Of course, Dawkins rejects any supernatural source of moral order, either an intrinsic moral order in creation or one issued by divine command. So, we are still at a loss as to the source of the morality by which Dawkins thinks he can condemn Christianity. Odd as it sounds, we'll have a better understanding of Dawkins' attempts to put forth his own version of morality if we look at his reasons for rejecting a revealed source of morality, which for the most part boils down to his rejection of a Biblical source of morality. Again, we remind the reader of St. Thomas' dictum that believers don't defend the Bible against non-believers by appealing to the Bible as authoritative. We intend to analyze his criticisms of the Bible on *his* own terms, even though, on our own terms of faith, we would never characterize the Bible as Dawkins does or we are about to do. Our goal is solely to illuminate Dawkins' moral stand as it emerges through his criticism of what he finds immoral in the Bible.

"The God of the Old Testament is arguably the most unpleasant character in all fiction: jealous and proud of it; a petty, unjust, unforgiv-

ing control-freak; a vindictive, bloodthirsty ethnic cleanser; a misogy-
nistic, homophobic, racist, infanticidal, genocidal, filicidal, pestilential,
megalomaniacal, sadomasochistic, capriciously malevolent bully."[1] So
begins Dawkins' argument against God in *The God Delusion*. Although
he lets off his attack upon the biblical God for a bit, by chapter seven,
having dispatched the supernatural designer, he's ready to take on the
God of the Old Testament.

Dawkins lists a number of objectionable Old Testament scenes:
Lot's offering of his two daughters to the men of Sodom who want
to rape his two male houseguests (Gen. 19:4–11), the incest of Lot's
daughters (Gen. 19:30–38), the near sacrifice of Isaac by his father
Abraham (Gen. 22:1–19), Moses' slaughter of 3000 Israelites after finding they had made a golden calf while he was up on Mt. Sinai getting
the Ten Commandments (Ex. 32:25–29), God's command to massacre
the Midianites (Num. 31:17–18), Joshua's putting all of the inhabitants
of Jericho to the sword (Josh 6:21), and God's "rules" for waging holy
war in Canaan (Dt. 20:10–18). In regard to the last two, he remarks
that Joshua's destruction of Jericho and the "invasion" of the Promised
Land thereafter is "morally indistinguishable from Hitler's invasion of
Poland, or Saddam Hussein's massacres of Kurds and the Marsh Ar-
abs." Taking over the Promised Land meant genocide, killing of all the
men, and carrying the women off for breeding.[2]

But precisely here problems arise for Dawkins' argument. Suppose
upon reading his devastating attack on the God of the Old Testament,
we would reject the Bible and embrace Dawkins' atheism—exactly what
Dawkins wishes to be the effect on readers. What then?

---

1    Richard Dawkins, *The God Delusion*, 31.
2    Richard Dawkins, *The God Delusion*, 247. Dawkins' complaints against the Old Testament
     occur in chapter 7, 239–250.

First of all, as we've already noted, in coming over to Dawkins' side, we have thereby embraced a cosmos indifferent to good or evil. As a consequence, we immediately face a dilemma: we have no moral grounds for condemning the actions of God (He doesn't exist) or the characters in the Bible (good and evil don't exist). Since God doesn't exist, there is no reason to work up a froth of indignation against Him, anymore than against the lunkheaded Zeus in Homer's *Iliad*. Obviously, the indignation, on whatever grounds Dawkins may have it, must be directed at the historical people represented in the Bible and in turn the people who believe the text to be holy.

Yet now another, more amusing problem arises. It would seem that a good many of the complaints made by Dawkins against the God of the Old Testament could, with equal justice, be made against natural selection itself. That is, the very complaints that bring him to reject the Old Testament are the ones that brought him to reject Darwinism itself as a moral foundation and guide. To say the least, he puts himself in a paradoxical position.

If we might put it in an arresting way, many sociologists of religion argue that primitive people tend to fashion their notions of the gods according to the way they experience nature, as nature deified (whether this is true or not, we won't decide here, but will take it on trust for the purposes of illustration). What would evolution look like if we tried to deify evolution's principles? Would the Evolution God (EG) be "unjust" in its callous indifference "to all suffering," and supremely so, for continually picking off the weak and sickly? Would EG be an "unforgiving control-freak," "megalomaniacal," and "petty" since (as Darwin stated), "It may metaphorically be said that natural selection is daily and hourly scrutinising, throughout the world, the slightest variations; rejecting those that are bad, preserving and adding up all that are good; silently and insensibly working, *whenever and wherever opportunity offers*, at the improvement of each organic being in relation to its organic and inorganic conditions of life"?[3] Would EG be "sadomasochistic" in its use of suffering, destruction, and death as the means to create new forms of life? A "capriciously malevolent bully" in his "lacking all purpose" and being "callous"? A "bloodthirsty ethnic cleanser," "genocidal," and "racist" in his continually pitting one species population against another in severe struggle, the struggles among humans taking place between tribe and tribe, race and race? And what adjective would describe EG, who uses these deadly struggles as the very vehicle responsible for the upward climb of human evolution?

So we've rejected the God of the Old Testament for Dawkins' atheistic account of evolution, only to find out that many of the traits Dawkins marked as repugnant are ensconced in natural selection (except that now, as a new and even more unfortunate kind of Job, we have no one against whom to complain).

Perhaps Dawkins will fare better in his case against the people of the Old Testament? But now another paradox comes to the fore. It would be hard to imagine a people who more assiduously pursued a better set of evolutionary strategies for ensuring that its gene pool was carried forward, undiluted by rival tribes and races, than the ancient Jews. They were genetic geniuses.

Think over the above reprehensible examples Dawkins provided from the Bible and then ruminate upon his account of how evolution, including human evolution, works. Dawkins maintains in his *Selfish Gene* that we may "treat the individual as a selfish machine, programmed to do whatever is best for its genes as a whole" (although, as he makes clear, the invisible level of the struggle between genes in a single individual is, for him, the real level of natural selection and the struggle to survive).

---

3    Charles Darwin, *The Origin of Species*, Chapter IV, "Natural Selection," p. 91.

The selfish machine works, literally, by gene-o-cide, the destruction and use of other selfish machines, treating them as fodder for its own survival. For a survival machine, "another survival machine (which is not its own child or another close relative) is part of its environment, like a rock or a river or a lump of food. It is something that gets in the way, or something that can be exploited....Natural selection favours genes that control their survival machines in such a way that they make the best use of the environment. This includes making the best use of other survival machines, both of the same and of different species."[4]

So what *exactly* did the ancient Israelites do wrong, evolutionarily speaking, in wiping out the other tribes in the Holy Land and in jealously protecting against intermarriage? It is very difficult to say, since both Darwin and Dawkins agree that the severity of the evolutionary struggle intensifies the more alike are two species that occupy the same territory (say, similar Semitic "species" in Canaan), with the greatest severity occurring between members of the same species (say, Moses vs. the calf-makers in Exodus, or vs. Miriam and Aaron in Numbers 12, or vs. Korah in Numbers 16).

Further, as Dawkins tells us, such survival machines, especially the males, are particularly set on snatching females for reproduction purposes, thereby creating continual conflict. In this conflict, survival is the rule for survival machines, and that includes especially the successful struggle for mates. For this reason, "a male might benefit his own genes if he does something detrimental to another male with whom he is competing."[5]

Above, we noted Dawkins' excoriation of Moses for commanding the Israelites entering the Promised Land to kill all the males and carry off the women. This certainly seems to be good evolutionary policy.

---

4   Richard Dawkins, *The Selfish Gene*, 66.
5   Richard Dawkins, *The Selfish Gene*, 67.

And the whole strange fascination with the Promised Land?—well, as Dawkins points out, the defense of territory is part of good Darwinian strategy: "Many animals devote a great deal of time and energy to apparently defending an area of ground which naturalists call a territory....In many cases females refuse to mate with males who do not possess a territory. Indeed it often happens that a female whose mate is defeated and his territory conquered promptly attaches herself to the victor....If the population gets too big, some individuals will not get territories, and therefore will not breed. Winning a territory is therefore...like winning a ticket or license to breed."[6]

The reader gets the point. Nearly everything that Dawkins complains about in regard to the Israelites either occurs among animals of other species, or fulfills admirably some kind of evolutionary strategy expressed in other species engaged as they are in the struggle to survive. From Dawkins' perspective, since human beings are one more kind of animal, it is hard to fault the Israelites for being lean, mean survival machines.

Again, we remind ourselves that Dawkins explicitly denies that we should use Darwin's *Origin of Species* and *Descent of Man*, or his own *Selfish Gene*, as moral guidebooks. But now we realize that, oddly enough, the *Origin, Descent,* and *Selfish Gene* stand in the same position as the Bible (or at least the Old Testament) for Dawkins: *none of them* should be used for moral guidelines, and for much the same reasons.

There now arises an illuminating connection between Dawkins and the believers he criticizes. Dawkins is not making the case that modern Christians *do* act like the people in the Old Testament as he describes them. Rather, he wants to make clear that what believers actually do is "pick and choose among the scriptures for the nice bits and reject the nasty." But if such is the case, adds Dawkins, believers must

---

6    Richard Dawkins, *The Selfish Gene*, 113.

be using some kind of independent criterion "for deciding which are the moral bits," which, since they apparently don't come from Scripture, must be available for non-believers as well.[7] As will become apparent, Dawkins does the exact same thing in regard to evolution (and so, we assume, has some independent criterion as well).

But before we analyze this point further, we should finish Dawkins' treatment of the Bible. Interestingly enough, he deals with the New Testament differently than the Old. Dawkins regards Jesus as one of the great ethical innovators of history, singling out especially the Sermon on the Mount. "It was not for nothing that I wrote an article called 'Atheists for Jesus.'"[8] In this revealing article, Dawkins asserts that Jesus was

> ...a theist because, in his time, everybody was. Atheism was not an option, even for so radical a thinker as Jesus. What was interesting and remarkable about Jesus was not the obvious fact that he believed in the God of his Jewish religion, but that he rebelled against many aspects of Yahweh's vengeful nastiness. At least in the teachings that are attributed to him, he publicly advocated niceness and was one of the first to do so. To those steeped in the Sharia-like cruelties of Leviticus and Deuteronomy; to those brought up to fear the vindictive, Ayatollah-like God of Abraham and Isaac, a charismatic young preacher who advocated generous forgiveness must have seemed radical to the point of subversion. No wonder they nailed him.[9]

In fact, Jesus was so "nice," that he can't help feeling that, underneath it all, he must really be...well...a lot like Richard Dawkins.

---

7   Richard Dawkins, *The God Delusion*, 243.
8   Richard Dawkins, *The God Delusion*, 250.
9   This essay is available on Dawkins' own website: http://richarddawkins.net/article,20,Atheists-for-Jesus,Richard-Dawkins.

I think a reborn Jesus would wear the T-shirt ["Atheists for Jesus"]. It has become a commonplace that, were he to return today, he would be appalled at what is being done in his name, by Christians ranging from the Catholic Church to the fundamentalist Religious Right. Less obviously but still plausibly, in the light of modern scientific knowledge I think he would see through supernaturalist obscurantism. But of course, modesty would compel him to turn his T-shirt around: Jesus for Atheists.[10]

Setting aside the stranger aspects of these ruminations, we may see that for Dawkins the "moral superiority of Jesus" proves a deeper point about Scripture. "Jesus was not content to derive his ethics from the scriptures of his upbringing [i.e., the Old Testament]. He explicitly departed from them," which goes to show that "we do not, and should not, derive our morals from scripture," and further, that "Jesus has to be honoured as a model for that very thesis."[11]

But as Dawkins makes equally clear in the same article, "Atheists for Jesus," wherever Jesus got his ethics, it wasn't from natural selection. "Natural selection is a deeply nasty process. Darwin himself remarked, 'What a book a devil's chaplain might write on the clumsy, wasteful, blundering low and horribly cruel works of nature.'" The problem is that the "theory of natural selection itself seems calculated to foster selfishness at the expense of public good, violence, callous indifference to suffering, short term greed at the expense of long term foresight." It doesn't get us the "super niceness" advocated by Jesus, desired by Dawkins, and instantiated (as Dawkins relates) in some of his friends. Sounding like Darwin himself in his wrestling with the tug of "hard

10  Richard Dawkins, "Atheists for Jesus."
11  Richard Dawkins, *The God Delusion*, 250.

reason," Dawkins confesses that "from a rational choice point of view, or from a Darwinian point of view, human super niceness is just plain dumb."[12] Yet, Dawkins hopes that it may spread nonetheless.

The irony is palpable. Dawkins' entire life is devoted to evolutionary evangelization, but evolution is immoral (or, at least, not nice, but more like the Old Testament God he excoriates). Like Jesus, Dawkins is "not content to derive his ethics from the scriptures of his upbringing," which for Dawkins would be the collective revelations of the Moses of evolution, Charles Darwin, taken down in his *Origin of Species* and *Descent of Man*. Instead, just like Christians, he asserts that some new moral principles supercede the evidently repugnant moral lessons one would (and many did) draw from the "Old Testament" of Darwin and from "fallen" nature itself. Yet, as it turns out, Dawkins does not simply reject all the moral implications of evolution, but rather "picks and chooses," taking the nice bits and rejecting the nasty.

This gives us the answer to our question, where does Dawkins get *his* independent moral criteria? He picks and chooses them from evolution, or more accurately, from Dawkins himself, as can be seen in his attempt to pick and choose from evolution those moral traits that he himself for some reason finds congenial: kindness, altruism, generosity, empathy, pity, and compassion.[13] We assume all these go together to make up "super niceness."

The difficulty, of course, is not with the traits he finds congenial. A Christian should affirm them as well. The difficulty for Dawkins lies in the fact that these "nice" traits are derived from evolution, and hence not themselves any more "moral" than the "nasty" traits that likewise contribute to survival. He himself is picking and choosing from the great multiplicity of evolutionary traits, the par-

---

12  Richard Dawkins, "Atheists for Jesus."
13  Richard Dawkins, *The God Delusion*, 221.

ticular traits that he, Richard Dawkins, would *like* to be moral, and hence would *like* to be universal. But that means, as he admits, leaving the other "nasty" traits behind.

How to get to super niceness or something close out of the mixed moral bag of evolution? First, he gives an evolutionary explanation of the traits he admires. Dawkins makes a case for other animals of something like a four-fold development of altruism, claiming that he has provided "four good Darwinian reasons for individuals to be altruistic, generous or 'moral' towards each other."[14] The scare quotes around moral attest to the need to distinguish between the evolution of a beneficial trait, and the consideration of it as moral. In regard to human beings, he asserts that a similar account can be given for the human animal. (His account of the evolution of altruism is very similar to Darwin's account of the evolution of sympathy and functions much the same way.)

The problem is, as Dawkins admits, that these could not have been universally-expressed traits: "our prehistoric ancestors would have been good to their own in-group but bad—to the point of xenophobia—towards other groups." The problem, to put it more exactly, is that even if we give an evolutionary account of altruism, it only extends to one's own group. It is tribal-centric, or at best, ethno-centric, and that brings us back to the Old Testament. His complaint against the "ethnic cleansing" in the Bible and the xenophobia of the Israelites, which fueled it, seems, then, to be entirely misplaced.[15] The ancient Jews were simply acting within the natural circuit of evolution: they were altruistic to their own kind and savage toward their enemies. They perfectly illustrate Dawkins' description of the evolutionary development of altruism. Evolution is to blame, not religion.

14  Richard Dawkins, *The God Delusion*, 219.
15  Richard Dawkins, *The God Delusion*, 247.

This makes Dawkins' charge against religion highly dubious: to complain that religion is the main cause of in-group, out-group conflict is merely to complain that it is Darwinian. He bids the reader to look at any violent arena in our world today, remarking that it is a good bet that religion is the cause, with religious differences defining the in-group, out-group distinctions.[16] But as he himself argued, evolution tells us that the *original* cause of in-group, out-group conflict is the struggle between rival genetic, or ethnic populations. Different religions, arriving historically after the rise of the ethnic differences, could certainly exacerbate the animosity and make labeling easier, but the leading cause (in both senses) is entirely explainable as due to the normal workings of evolution. But if such is the case, then for Dawkins, they are neither good nor evil any more than the equivalent struggles of other species that go on all the time. That's just how nature works.

So we see why, on Dawkins' terms and by his own admission, altruism isn't universal. The truth of this is obvious enough from the list of nasty conflicts going on now in the world that Dawkins rightly laments. The question for a good atheistic evolutionist like Dawkins, then, is: Why do some people act *as if* altruism were directed at *all* human beings rather than their own genetic in-group?

As he makes clear, when certain individuals act as if altruism, or kindness, generosity, empathy, and pity are universal, these acts are actually kinds of evolutionary "misfirings, Darwinian mistakes: blessed, precious mistakes."[17] For Dawkins, the trait (altruism) has become, strangely enough, detached from its original, quite particular object (the in-group), as if a particular bird somehow had gone batty and started indiscriminately caring for *all* young of any kind rather than the young of its *own* kind. While he hopes that these precious "misfirings" can

16 Richard Dawkins, *The God Delusion*, 260.
17 Richard Dawkins, *The God Delusion*, 221.

somehow be universalized, he has to admit that their evolutionary development would have *depended upon* their rise and nurturing among so-called xenophobic tribes, and also that as misfirings they have no support from natural selection (and as isolated instances would likely evaporate from the gene pool soon enough). In either case, no one can be blamed for acting against such misfirings.

Whatever Dawkins' wistful notions of super niceness, a casual look at the 20th and now the 21st century would seem to support that ethnic xenophobia, and hence bloody conflict, is more in evidence than a sustained outbreak of altruism. Again, since ethnicity almost invariably has far deeper roots historically than the religions that are now attached to ethnic differences, then the miserable contemporary conflicts lamented by Dawkins are far more likely to be Darwinian in essence. Whether one agrees with this point or not, certainly no sane evolutionist could assume from the baleful evidence available that altruism had *in fact* become detached from its in-group moorings and begun to spread; only that he *wishes* it would. And in this respect, Dawkins seems to be a sane evolutionist. As he says in "Atheists for Jesus," we need to "lead society away from the nether regions of its Darwinian origins into kinder and more compassionate uplands."

Yet, such sanity leads to further irony. The parallels between Dawkins and the Christians he berates seem all too evident, even though Dawkins misses or ignores them. Both believe that nature is somehow "fallen," not what it "should be," and Dawkins (despite his horror at the notion[18]) even has a quasi-equivalent concept of original sin, the selfish gene, that (just as St. Augustine said of original sin) is passed on through procreation. Both depend upon primary texts that act as revelations upon which everything else must build (Darwin's *Origin of Species* and *Descent of Man*, and the Old Testament), and both

---

18   Richard Dawkins, *The God Delusion*, 251.

look for a super-natural (above-natural) purification of what pertains in the original revelations and in nature (super niceness over Darwinian natural selection and Christ's transformation of the old law and the old nature in the New Testament). Both look at Christ as exemplary, although Dawkins avers that "I think we owe Jesus the honour of separating his genuinely original and radical ethics from the supernatural nonsense which he inevitably espoused as a man of his time."[19]

But even with these important similarities to Christianity in general and Jesus in particular, one may well wonder if there really is some deep, underlying moral vision that Dawkins shares with Christianity and Christ. The vision of "super niceness," which he believes that Jesus generally supported and would support even more fervently if only he had lived to be Richard Dawkins, is actually a pastiche of Christianity as filtered through 19th century liberalism (more or less what we would find in John Stuart Mill's *Utilitarianism*), and its radical extension, via Darwinism, into the farther reaches of 21st century liberalism. This ethical vision, Dawkins maintains, is "a somewhat mysterious consensus," that is apparently growing, which he calls "the moral *Zeitgeist*," the "moral spirit of the times."[20] In this *geist* Dawkins places all his moral hopes for the future. But just how moral is this *geist*? To that question, we shall turn in the next chapter.

---

19  Richard Dawkins, "Atheists for Jesus."
20  Richard Dawkins, *The God Delusion*, 262–272.

# 7

# DAWKINS DISMANTLED

No more Mr. Nice Guy.

By Dawkins' own admission, he invokes "super niceness" as a kind of moral goal that, while it may have some original traces in the evolution of altruism, is ultimately defined against our evolutionary origin. Given his approving words about the ethics of Jesus, it would seem that, although he began at a radically different cosmological beginning, he ends up at roughly the same moral end as Christians.

What is the source of this alleged commonality? And more importantly, is there really common moral ground between Dawkins and Christianity? He makes some effort to show that there is common ground, although the argument is in the service of his belief that since there is common moral ground, then "we do not need God in order to be good—or evil."[1]

Dawkins offers one proof of common ground in a study that revealed that people from many different cultures give roughly the same responses to contrived moral dilemmas (very contrived, we should note: the dubious runaway-trolley-with-several-people-on-the-tracks-and-will-you-throw-the-switch-if-it-diverts-the-train-into-another-innocent-bystander type quandaries). His conclusion: since atheists, believers, and non-Westerners give about

---

1   Richard Dawkins, *The God Delusion*, 226.

the same responses, then evolution must have been the cause of uniformity, not religion.[2] (Peter Singer was one of the atheist philosophers who defined and administered the study testing the moral responses of atheists and religious people—an ironic point, as we'll see below, that undermines the entire study.[3]) This conclusion is bolstered by the "fact" that Christians pick and choose what is moral from Scripture, rather than having Scripture determine for them what is moral.[4]

Evolution, then, provides something of a common moral sense, and in fact, grounds a common human nature that allows for a common moral foundation. In fact, claims Dawkins, recognition of a common human nature is being carried forward against the grain of religion by the moral *Zeitgeist*, something that Dawkins argues does not come from the Bible, but from biology, especially evolution.[5]

Although Dawkins isn't quite clear, we assume that the ethics of Jesus, super niceness, and the advancing moral *Zeitgeist* march more or less together. He is also not clear how we sort out having a common humanity on one end, and races of human beings branching off into different species on the other.

However, even though he fails to sort all that out, he happily maintains that we now enjoy a growing "broad liberal consensus of ethical principles." Most of us won't cause needless suffering, we believe in free speech, we pay taxes, we don't cheat, kill, or commit incest, and we generally follow the golden rule.[6]

While this might all look fairly cheery—so that there is no radical moral disagreement between Christians and atheists—a closer look reveals otherwise. Despite the surface similarity, the fundamental dis-

2   Richard Dawkins, *The God Delusion*, 222–225.
3   Richard Dawkins, *The God Delusion*, 225.
4   Richard Dawkins, *The God Delusion*, 249, 255, 262.
5   Richard Dawkins, *The God Delusion*, 271.
6   Richard Dawkins, *The God Delusion*, 263.

agreement that exists between a universe with and without a super-natural Creator also manifests those fundamental differences in rival, irreconcilable moral views.

From very early on, Christianity has been adamantly against abortion and infanticide, as one of the earliest non-New Testament documents, the *Didache*, unambiguously attests. "You shall not slaughter a child in abortion nor slay a begotten one." This prohibition was obviously part of the general prohibition, "Do not kill."[7] Further, as we noted above, the prohibition itself was rooted in the biblical understanding that all human beings were created in the image of God.

While Dawkins accepts the general admonition not to kill, when it comes to concrete instances where one must decide whether a particular act violates the prohibition "Do not kill," his veneer of common morality easily tears away. This is accomplished, in some instances, by jettisoning the notion of a common humanity. For example, in regard to abortion, Dawkins asks rhetorically, "given that the embryo lacks a nervous system, shouldn't the mother's well-developed nervous system have the choice?"[8] And late term abortions? Well, reasons Dawkins, if late-term aborted embryos suffer, "it is not because they are *human* that they suffer." Indeed, no embryo at any age would seem to suffer more than a cow or sheep embryo at the same stage of development. And in fact, claims Dawkins, adult cows or sheep in the slaughterhouse certainly suffer more than any embryo, human or not.[9]

So, as it ends up, just after championing our common humanity as the sure ground of the new moral *Zeitgeist*, Dawkins asserts that secular moralists do not ask whether an embryo is a human, but instead focus on the quantity of suffering: "'Never mind whether it is *human* (what

7   Philip Schaff, *Teaching of the Twelve Apostles* (New York: Funk & Wagnalls, 1885), 2.2, pp. 168–169. Our translation.
8   Richard Dawkins, *The God Delusion*, 293.
9   Richard Dawkins, *The God Delusion*, 297.

does that even *mean* for a little cluster of cells?); at what age does any developing embryo, of any species, become capable of *suffering?*"[10]

In reasoning thusly, Dawkins is showing his indebtedness not only to Darwin, but to John Stuart Mill's secular liberal theory of Utilitarianism. In accordance with Mill's Utilitarianism (which, as Mill himself admitted, was simply an updated form of ancient Epicureanism), ethics is rooted, not in a common humanity (as Dawkins seems to infer), but in the maximization of pleasure and minimization of pain. The difficulty with this type of ethical theory, as Dawkins happily points out, is that a full-grown animal might indeed suffer more than a child in the womb, or even a small child out of the womb. In fact, there is no reason to prefer human beings morally *at all*. Whatever suffers more, is thereby morally superior. If such is the case, human beings should receive no moral preference over equally or more developed animals.

In this regard, Dawkins praises the evolutionist and atheist "philosopher Peter Singer" as the most eloquent advocate against the speciesist notion that human beings are somehow morally superior. For Singer, all species with significant "brain power" should be treated the same morally.[11] While this may be big-hearted, practically speaking, it ends up rather morally macabre, because it really means treating human beings like other animals. In Singer's *Practical Ethics*—the *first* edition—Singer happily confided that "not...everything the Nazis did was horrendous; we cannot condemn euthanasia just because the Nazis did it."[12] The second edition had this expunged, but did not take out Singer's unblinking advocacy of euthanasia and its extension to infanticide, not just to relieve any alleged "suffering" of the infant, but even more, for the

---

10   Richard Dawkins, *The God Delusion*, 297–298. Dawkins is quoting someone else here with approval.

11   Richard Dawkins, *The God Delusion*, 271.

12   Peter Singer, *Practical Ethics* (Cambridge: Cambridge University Press, 1979), 124. For a short account of Singer see Donald DeMarco and Benjamin Wiker, *Architects of the Culture of Death* (San Francisco: Ignatius Press, 2004), 361–373.

sake of any hesitations of the parents over keeping their newborn. Just as with the Nazis, Singer would allow the retarded, the feeble-minded, the handicapped, in short, all the unfit, to be exterminated without a twinge of conscience. That is how we treat other animals when they have disabilities and deformities. We can now see the irony of Singer being the co-author of a study that determined that religious people and atheists have pretty much the same moral views.

Dawkins, too, is quite clear in his advocacy of euthanasia,[13] although more cryptic in what that might imply. He seems to make it morally acceptable as a personal decision about one's own life. The problem is that the person loudly proclaiming the right to put himself out of his own misery will soon enough, like Singer, claim the right to put others out of his misery as well. This is not an empty prophecy. In the Netherlands, the legalization of euthanasia quickly led to the involuntary euthanasia of the elderly, the sick, and infants.

On the positive end of extending our relationship with other animals, Singer is perfectly cheerful about bestiality—provided, of course, that one in no way causes the animal to suffer during the experience, for "sex with animals does not always involve cruelty."[14]

Does that mean that Dawkins agrees that the zeitgeist will wend its way to the acceptance of bestiality? It is difficult to tell. Dawkins offers his own amendments to the various attempts by like-minded folk to write a new and improved Ten Commandments, the first amendment being, "Enjoy your own sex life (so long as it damages nobody else) and leave others to enjoy theirs in private whatever their inclinations, which are none of your business."[15] What does "whatever" include? But let us assume, we hope rightly, that he does not find acceptable Singer's approval

---

13  Richard Dawkins, *The God Delusion*, 357.
14  Peter Singer, "Heavy Petting," a review of Midas Dekkers, *Dearest Pet: On Bestiality* (New York: Verso, 2000). Singer's infamous review is available at many different locations on the internet.
15  Richard Dawkins, *The God Delusion*, 264.

of bestiality. Even so, he is faced with a problem of principle. Given that both he and Singer work according to the same principle—that species distinctions are morally insignificant and that morality must therefore be determined by the capacity to feel pleasure and pain—Dawkins cannot offer a good reason that Singer's affirmation of bestiality is illicit. Such would seem to be the inevitable result if, in accordance with the kind of Darwinism Dawkins espouses, one erases the species distinction that makes human beings morally significant and places them on a spectrum of other sentient beings, making the ability to feel pleasure and pain the focus of moral decisions.

As should be clear, the problem with atheism (at least of Dawkins' and Singer's kind) is not that (riffing Dostoyevsky) "all is permitted." The problem must be situated within the particular history of the secularization of the Christian West. The real problem is that certain things that had not been permitted when people believed in the Christian God will be at first permitted and then mandated. Laws against euthanasia will become laws permitting euthanasia, which will then be superceded by laws mandating euthanasia.

Such is the ambiguous nature of "super niceness" blown in by Dawkins' *zeitgeist*. It shows us why the list of moral traits—kindness, altruism, generosity, empathy, pity, and compassion—espoused by Dawkins are at best vague and, at worst, entirely misleading for most people who read his book. Kindness means two different things in two different moral universes. For the Christian, it would mean palliative care for the dying but (since human beings have immortal souls, and hence differ fundamentally from other animals) it also means that euthanasia would be forbidden. For Dawkins, since we are animals without souls and an eternal destiny, kindness means having medical euthanasia for human beings available as the same kind of humane treatment we give to animals at the veterinarian's. But, as we've seen with Singer (in theory) and the Netherlands (in practice), since we put down diseased and malformed animals, we may also put down diseased and malformed human beings. Whether Dawkins would agree with this extension or not, Singer has correctly inferred it from the same principles Dawkins espouses.

The same is true with the other moral traits as they bear on particular moral issues, for example, abortion. Generosity for the Christian would mean adopting an unwanted child or providing shelter to pregnant women; for Dawkins, generosity would mean supporting or providing abortion services. Clearly, then, agreement on the prohibition "Do not kill" does not translate into moral agreement on concrete issues like abortion, and adding the general admonition that we should all be generous does nothing to resolve moral disagreements about such particular issues.

Therefore, in understanding what is at stake in this great debate, we must continually keep in mind that similarity of moral language often masks utter irreconcilability of moral content. Another example. Dawkins speaks favorably of compassion. This leaves Christian readers with the false assumption that "compassion" means the same thing for them as it does for Dawkins. But what "compassion" means for Dawkins and what it means for the Christian is, all too often, entirely the opposite. For Dawkins, compassion entails euthanasia; for the Christian, euthanasia is a species of murder. For Singer, compassion means killing a retarded newborn; for the Christian, that is infanticide.

We can now see that at the very deepest root of these moral disagreements is a fundamental and irreconcilable disagreement about human nature, and no one speaks to this point more eloquently and exactly than Dawkins himself. As he makes clear, the notion of "humanness" can carry no moral weight precisely because of our evolutionary continuity with other species. If all the missing links that connect us to our simian ancestors could be dug up—or better, had survived—and human beings were placed among them on the evolutionary spectrum, it would be difficult if not impossible to distinguish the last ape from the first man. In Dawkins' words, "the gradual continuity that is an inescapable feature of biological evolution tells us that there must be *some* intermediate who would lie sufficiently close to the 'borderline' to blur the moral principle and destroy its absoluteness." For Dawkins, that means that "absolutist moral discrimination [as is found in Christianity and certain other religions] is devastatingly undermined by the fact of evolution." He conjectures that believers realize this, and hence they reject evolution because they fear that it wipes out moral distinctions. "They are wrong to do so," however.[16]

We have already seen Dawkins' unqualified affirmation of abortion and euthanasia, and the evolutionist Singer's approval of infanticide and bestiality. Can Christians take seriously Dawkins' statement that they have nothing to fear concerning the moral implications of evolution?

We should now have no doubt that Dawkins' denial of any species distinction goes to the heart of the moral divide between his moral *Zeitgeist* and the moral spirit of Christianity, and why this must end in spiritual combat. Again, "Don't kill" as a divine commandment is grounded in the belief that human beings are fundamentally distinct from all other animals; that they are made in the image of God. The commandment isn't "Don't kill any living thing" but "Don't kill any innocent human being." If the species distinction is blurred then we get two sorts of results. The first is an *indefinite extension* of the principle: "Don't kill human beings and chimpanzees, gorillas, orangutans, or antelopes, aardvarks, ants...and zebras" Why? The very continuity of the species (assum-

---

16  Richard Dawkins, *The God Delusion*, 300–301.

ing the countless intermediates) ensures that *any* attempt to draw a moral line in regard to killing is undermined by the fact of evolution. Dawkins' meager attempt to draw a line above (suggesting that humane treatment should be dealt out to all species that have the brain power to appreciate it) is undermined by the obvious difficulty of determining "brain power" and "appreciate" on a seamless continuum of evolution.

A second possibility is an *indefinite retraction* of the principle. When "Don't kill" applied only to human beings, the inference was that killing (and eating) non-human sentient creatures was perfectly moral. But as soon as the moral status of human beings is removed, there is no reason to continue the prohibition. Nor should we irrationally prohibit any use of the human animal that we had previously allowed for other animals. *Any* use, from medicinal to culinary.

Again, we are not attempting to convict Richard Dawkins of cannibalism. Our argument is about principles, not persons. Whatever his inclinations, cannibalism occurs throughout the animal kingdom and is historically found among many cultures. From an evolutionary point of view, there is no reason to condemn it. First of all, evolution does not condemn any moral trait, but can only explain it. Second, cannibalism is only a bad evolutionary strategy if it is confined to one's immediate in-group. Third, the principles of liberalism or super niceness do not preclude using human flesh for all kinds of purposes, as should already be quite clear from the current and expanding use of human embryos for every kind of medicinal purpose, a more elaborate form of cannibalism.

So, however much Dawkins wishes to assure his religious readers that they have nothing to fear from his atheism, a closer inspection yields the frightening conclusion that what to the Christian marks the onset of a great moral darkness is for Dawkins the light of his moral *Zeitgeist*. Even without determining which is correct, we can see their fundamental conflict.

# 8

# KING RICHARD

## What would Dawkins do?

If anything is clear from our inquiry into the arguments of Richard Dawkins' *The God Delusion*, it is this: the debate about whether or not God exists is both a theoretical *and* moral debate. Or, if we might put it this way, a good part of Dawkins' urgency and undisguised animosity in *The God Delusion* arises from his conviction that Christians are under a *moral* delusion as well. For him, Christians are fundamentally irrational, and the fundamental irrationally plays itself out morally in the public sphere. He is not just worried about Muslims blowing up buildings but also about Christians attempting to push through legislation against abortion, euthanasia, homosexuality, and so on. From his point of view—and we must remember that this is a *worldview*—Christianity is morally pernicious. And as Dawkins makes clear, he is just as worried about mild and moderate forms of faith as he is about religious extremism because even moderate forms allow for the existence of extreme forms.[1]

But Dawkins goes further, calling the religious instruction of children "child abuse." His reasoning is quite simple. Since all religions are false, it is a form of child abuse to indoctrinate children with beliefs that they can't possibly question. For Dawkins,

---

1    Richard Dawkins, *The God Delusion*, 303.

child sex abuse by the clergy is bad enough, but far worse is "the long-term psychological damage inflicted by bringing the child up Catholic in the first place."[2] Not the least of the damage done is the inculcation of the notion that there is a hell.

Dawkins makes the charge of child abuse with all seriousness, and this brings him to wade into what even he regards as dangerous waters. If it is abuse, then shouldn't children be protected *from* their parents? Agreeing heartily with psychologist Nicholas Humphrey, Dawkins argues against the notion that parents have a right to educate their own children in their own faith, precisely because children have a right to be protected from harmful nonsense. The children's right—much to the shock of his fellow liberal colleagues—must trump any notion of fostering cultural diversity, because that diversity includes the various religions against which children must be protected.[3] While Dawkins tags on a bit at the end about needing a kind of cultural-biblical education so as to understand literary references, the message is clear. Something must be done. After all, as we recall, Dawkins considers religion to be a mind virus.

What to make of it all? We'd like to end this book with a thought experiment, one that might help us understand where the debate is headed. There should be no doubt in the reader's mind by now that Dawkins and his ilk are planning a cultural revolution. They consider religion to be pernicious, and they want something done about it. Their arguments against religion are not meant to stay in the politically ineffectual lecture hall or reside only between the pages of their books. The new atheists are issuing an urgent call to action. What they lack is not atheistic chutzpah; they lack political power.

---

2    Richard Dawkins, *The God Delusion*, 317.
3    Richard Dawkins, *The God Delusion*, 325–331.

And so here is the thought experiment. If Richard were King, what would King Richard do? We offer this not as a personal analysis of his own proclivities, but in the following spirit: if Dawkins is in fact right about what he says, what would be the *reasonable* thing to do? This is not a merely theoretical experiment. When Lenin and the Bolsheviks gained power in the October Revolution of 1917, they were suddenly faced with the opportunity to put their merely theoretical Marxism into practice. They had to move from treating atheism as a theory to defining it as public policy. Reviewing the deeds of Lenin's party, one learns far more about Marxism than he would in turgid debates in the lecture hall.

So we ask, if you thought that religion was indeed a mind virus, one which infected innocent children and caused adults to embrace harmful mythologies, what would be the reasonable thing to do? If Richard were King, certainly the first, most reasonable thing to do would be to outlaw all religious instruction, whether it be publicly or privately funded. This would obviously take a fair amount of coercion on the part of the state, given the depth and variety of religious beliefs and the tenacious hold that religion has on many families. Certainly, there would need to be the state-mandated, early-as-possible separation of children from parents, which could easily be accomplished by the provision of free state daycare for children six weeks and above. In these facilities, the earliest education in Darwinism could occur.

As the Bolsheviks discovered, merely removing religious instruction would not be enough, for religion manifests itself in a plethora of ways, some obvious and visible, others intangible. It wouldn't do much good to prohibit religious indoctrination of the young by parents, if the whole family is free to march off to church each Sunday. Closing the churches must go hand in hand with closing the religious schools. These churches would not have to be wasted, but could be turned into museums that would display the dangers of religion, as compared with the kind of enlightenment that atheism provides.

But religious buildings are only one of the most obvious ways that religion continues to insinuate itself in the culture. The very notion of special days—holidays, the word coming originally from holy days—must be erased and displaced, for they only serve to remind the faithful of their misbegotten origins. We would think it rational for King Richard, under direction of a committee of the likewise enlightened, to fashion new public holidays that help to wean the unenlightened from pernicious cultural-religious habits. Given the signal importance of Darwinism, especially as it has raised Dawkins' own consciousness,[4] the entire Darwinian worldview should define the way that people count their days and set about their celebrations.

Darwin's birthday, February 12, could become a national holiday, but it stands to reason that the new atheist order would need to reinterpret the most important Christian religious holidays as a way to break their hold. Perhaps Christmas, as it coincides roughly with the winter solstice, could be commemorated as the darkest time of human history, when superstition entered the world in an especially repugnant way, and then the calendar could lead up to Darwin Day on February 12 where, although it is still cold (for he was born into a time of superstition), yet the world had become noticeably lighter. This would be considered part of the sojourn to spring, and even the crucifixion on Good Friday could be celebrated as the entirely rational response of the Romans to the presence of superstition. Of course, the commemoration of Easter itself would have to be entirely quashed, or simply made, in a return to reasonable paganism, a celebration of fecundity, in particular the kind of overbreeding in nature that allows for severe struggle, and hence natural selection. So as not to awaken the wrong conclusions, it

4    Richard Dawkins, *The God Delusion*, 1, 3, 114-119.

could be made clear that overbreeding is irrational for human beings by instigating a tradition of having children receive candy-baskets with condoms in some of the plastic eggs.

As King Richard would soon find, a real revolution cannot sustain itself (especially during its early years) if the irrational criticisms of its enemies are allowed free play. At the heart of the new order is the central belief that Darwinism is unquestionably correct, and the very foundation of further enlightenment. As Dawkins has already made clear about religion, even the most moderate forms must be eliminated because their presence legitimates the extreme forms. The same principle would apply to debates about Darwinism: allowing any criticism, even and especially scientific criticism, would have to be carefully proscribed. Any rational doubts from the most eminent scientists would legitimate the entirely irrational doubts of every hair-brained fundamentalist, and all such doubt, now that evolutionary atheism grounds the political order, must be considered a kind of treason.

Before becoming king, Dawkins made us aware of the fundamental moral differences that arise between an atheistic evolutionary worldview and a Christian worldview. According to Dawkins, someone who believes that an embryo is a human being, must believe that abortion is murder; and if he believes abortion is murder, then it is rational for him to do anything to defend innocent life, even kill the abortionist. Since even the opinion that abortion is murder lends support to the notion that abortionists should be killed, then all opposition to abortion must be ruthlessly suppressed.

The same would go for opposition to euthanasia. On evolutionary grounds, administering euthanasia to human beings is no different than putting our animals down humanely at the veterinarian's. Those who treat euthanasia as a species of murder would therefore lend support to any religious fanatic with a gun.

Likewise with nearly all the Christian moral schema. For Dawkins, prohibitions regarding sex serve only to increase the world's misery. Since the only reasonable moral criterion for evolutionary ethics is the reduction of suffering, then the new order has a moral obligation to enhance sexual enjoyment even while it seeks to systematically exterminate all vestigial Christian beliefs about human sexuality.

On the positive end of things, Darwinism invites us to participate in the great creative power of nature and celebrate our own abilities to select those traits that fit best our vision of humanity. Since we are one more kind of animal, then it would make sense (as it did to the Darwinists in Europe and America in the late 19th and early 20th centuries) for those in power to encourage only the best to breed and to remove genetic malformations from the breeding pool. This would seem to be the kindest way to treat those who come after us to the maximum of health and the minimum of suffering. While this was done in a rather clumsy way by the Nazis, now that we have the technology to screen genetically in the womb (which will only advance), abortion can become the standard means to the same eugenic end.

We recall Dawkins focus on brain-power as a morally significant mark. One can imagine that, since the only remarkable distinction between animals and human beings is the superior intelligence of the latter, superior intelligence will itself take on the status of a moral distinction, where the lack of intelligence will be considered a malformation. In the early 20th century, there was a great eugenic crusade against the "feeble-minded," a term which (using the new Intelligence Tests) designated those with an IQ score of 70 or below. The eugenic reasoning was quite simple: those who differ from the most intelligent human beings (IQ 130–160) as much as the most intelligent animals differ from the person of average intelligence (IQ 100) are ripe for eugenic elimination.

The suggestions for elimination of the feeble-minded in the first heyday of Darwinian eugenicism ran the spectrum from not allowing the unfit to breed to killing them. Would King Richard support eugenics, and where would he be on that spectrum? He certainly realizes the question is a touchy one, as he so very recently revealed in Scotland's *Sunday Herald*.

---

In the 1920s and 1930s, scientists from both the political left and right would not have found the idea of designer babies particularly dangerous—though of course they would not have used that phrase. Today, I suspect that the idea is too dangerous for comfortable discussion, and my conjecture is that Adolf Hitler is responsible for the change.

Nobody wants to be caught agreeing with that monster, even in a single particular. The spectre of Hitler has led some scientists to stray from "ought" to "is" and deny that breeding for human qualities is even possible. But if you can breed cattle for milk yield, horses for running speed, and dogs for herding skill, why on Earth should it be impossible to breed humans for mathematical, musical or athletic ability? Objections such as "these are not one-dimensional abilities" apply equally to cows, horses and dogs and never stopped anybody in practice.

I wonder whether, some 60 years after Hitler's death, we might at least venture to ask what the moral difference is between breeding for musical ability and forcing a child to take music lessons. Or why it is acceptable to train fast runners and high jumpers but not to breed them. I can think of some answers, and they are good ones, which would probably end up persuading me. But hasn't the time come when we should stop being frightened even to put the question?[5]

What, then, would Dawkins do if he were king, and unrestrained by public opinion? Given that he seems likely to support breeding for more fit qualities (affirming it in just the language Darwin used), it would be highly unlikely (given his support for abortion), that he would have problems with the elimination of the unfit in the womb. Given his emphasis on defining humanity by brain-power, we could reasonably expect that, were Dawkins king, he might foster the elimination of the "feeble-minded" through ever more sophisticated in-womb genetic testing (as, even now, the retarded are likely to be killed by abortion as the result of pre-natal screening), and perhaps even go as far as Peter Singer suggests, and legalize the elimination of the retarded by infanticide. The difference with the current situation would be this: once we believe that we have a moral obligation to remove the unfit, it will soon become a matter of the obligation for the state. One might reasonably venture that, for King Richard, such eugenics would perhaps be part of his larger vision of healthcare.

While this may all seem fantastic, such would be the rational, inevitable result if Dawkins' "super niceness" became a political program and his moral *zeitgeist* was allowed to blow whither it will. Anyone who has read about the French Revolution and witnessed how quickly reason in rebellion against Christianity turned into terror, or who has studied the horrors of the Bolshevik attempts at freeing humanity from the chains of religion by force, cannot regard this exercise as merely theoretical. Jacobinism and Bolshevism can take new forms, and even now, there is more than a little resemblance between them and the contemporary

---

5   Richard Dawkins, "From the Afterward," *Sunday Herald* (Scotland), November 19, 2006. Available at http://www.sundayherald.com/life/people/display.var.1031440.0.eugenics_ may_not_be_bad.php"

apostles of political correctness. Dawkins is loosely connected with this latter group, planting his flag, as he tells the reader, with the liberalism of the moral *zeitgeist*. Even more frightening, he has abandoned three related aspects of liberalism, the absolute respect for freedom of speech, a commitment to the toleration of cultural diversity, and the rights of the parents against intrusions by the state.[6] That means that Dawkins has cast aside the very principles of liberalism that were designed to keep it from becoming a new form of totalitarianism. In the absence of principles of restraint, the only thing keeping us from the fulfillment of a new kind of tyranny is the absence of power on the part of those like Richard Dawkins, Daniel Dennett, Christopher Hitchens, and Sam Harris, the Four Horsemen of the new atheism. But as we recall, political power is the very thing they now seek.

---

6   Richard Dawkins, *The God Delusion*, ch. 9.